# *More* LAP QUILTING

## with Georgia Bonesteel

Oxmoor House

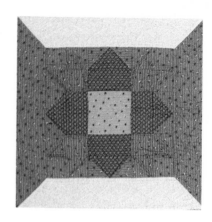

*To my sister Jill:*
>*Since I communicate through quilt making, capturing my techniques and thoughts on paper could have been a mountain of work. Jill, my personal word processor, helped me unscramble this book.*

*To Norma Thomas:*
>*She is more than just a secretary. She is a friend and quilt confidant.*

*To Shirley Klennon, Betsy Freeman, Frances Guardina, and Karen Pervier:*
>*These friends not only make quilts but* talk *quilts and* listen *to my quiltmania.*

*To the Western North Carolina Quilters Guild, the Landrum Library Quilters, the North Carolina Quilt Symposium Board, Inc., and the staff at Bonesteel's Hardware and Quilt Corner:*
>*We all have a common bond—to perpetuate and preserve the art of quilt making.*

*To Pete:*
>*Thank you for your understanding.*

Copyright 1985 Oxmoor House, Inc.
Book Division of Southern Progress Corporation
P.O. Box 2463, Birmingham, Alabama 35201

Library of Congress Catalog Number: 84-60287
ISBN: 0-8487-0634-X
Manufactured in the United States of America
First Printing 1985

*Pastel colors seem to explode in the sampler blocks that spin around the central spool motif in* Spinning Spools.

# Contents

# Introduction

When I excitedly announced to my family that I was going to write a sequel to *Lap Quilting* and tape another television series my daughter Amy asked, "But Mother, haven't you said it all? What else is there?" Why, Amy, there are more quilts, which means there are more patterns and more designs, and more techniques that I want to share with other quilters. So there has to be more...*More Lap Quilting*.

Lap quilting has provided a creative outlet for many people. As I travel around the country and meet other quilters, I am continually impressed by the popularity of lap quilting. Many of the quilters explain that before, quilting had seemed such an overwhelming task, but lap quilting has made it both possible and *plausible*.

Hearing this time and again reinforces and nurtures my enthusiasm for lap quilting. It has inspired me to design new quilts and develop more techniques and shortcuts for *More Lap Quilting*. In this book, you will find directions for new sampler quilts designed around center panels. Some of the panels are pieced but others are solid fabric. You will see how lap quilting can be adapted to diagonal settings and row lap-quilted. You will also see how an optional lap quilting technique lets you reverse the final handwork to the front instead of the back of the quilt.

When your mind clicks into its creative gear, it's amazing how it reaches out to make use of anything and everything around it. And it's amazing, too, how the crafts overlap. We quilters have chosen to cut cloth in pieces and reshape it into other patterns. But the designs and tools of other arts and crafts can be useful to us if we're on the lookout. For instance, one day I was wandering around a college bookstore when I came across a drafting tool used by architects, called a "flexible curve." For me, it produced a whole new idea in string piecing. I now call it the "flexicurve" and use it to sew and flip curves, in much less time than it would take me to appliqué each of the curves individually. I've also discovered new quick-piecing techniques that shorten time spent at the sewing machine. And new ideas in quilting give a creative look to your stitches.

*A quilted* Welcome Banner *is a perfect way to greet friends when they come to visit. This banner was made by adding borders to a Seldom Inn block.*

If you are in doubt about how much quilting to do, quilt more. When I compare my earlier quilts to today's, I find I'm doing more quilting now. That means I'm creating more interesting shadows. Be creative when deciding on your quilting lines, because they can be that special something that sets your quilt apart.

Several of the quilts and projects included were done with groups and guilds. I've included some helpful hints for those of you who are possibly considering establishing a new guild, and I've made suggestions on how to organize a guild project.

I hope all of you have had or will have the opportunity to quilt with a group. The stimulus and feedback from sharing is contagious. The expression "gallop and grin" in my first book came from just such a sharing experience. At one of our "show and tell" sessions we saw a very marginal error. The quilter was considering whether she should rip out her stitches and start over, when someone asked, "Would you see it on a galloping horse?" That, of course, made us all laugh; hence the expression, "gallop and grin."

Today I view lap quilting as an optional method for making a quilt. It's certainly not the only way, but one technique that has opened the door to quilting for many who might otherwise never have crossed the threshold.

Quilting is considered a sickness and a therapy at the same time. We often refer to someone for whom quilting is utterly consuming as having caught the quilting "bug." But there is also the theory that quilting is good therapy for idle hands and minds. If you have caught the bug or are still looking for excuses to quilt, remember, you are

- using that mountain of fabric you've collected
- creating the fiber history of tomorrow
- developing patience—"Inch by inch anything's a cinch"
- experiencing the satisfaction of creating a handmade gift
- going to sleep in style

And because it is so much fun and such a challenge we have discovered many other uses for the three-layered cloth—wall hangings, banners, vests, pillows, and tote bags—to mention just a few. May this new book, *More Lap Quilting,* be the springboard for your next quilt. Best wishes for small stitches.

### Quilting Fever

*It's really not a sickness.*
*When you catch the bug,*
*You look upon a quilt and*
*Feel your heart a-tug.*
*You suddenly get the urge*
*To try your hand at such,*
*And see how a quilt might look*
*Made with your own special touch.*
*You piece a block together*
*And cannot seem to stop.*
*You want to keep on sewing*
*Till you've finished the top.*
*You put the layers together*
*And start your needle through.*
*You finally get the hang of it,*
*Even though it's new.*
*Now you're really hooked*
*For you are the receiver*
*Of a fateful case of*
*"Quilting fever."*

—Charlotte Pierce

# Ready, Set, Sew

Once upon a time, after tripping over a gentleman as I stumbled into an airplane window seat, I was asked, "Do you always carry your toaster oven with you?" "No," I replied, "but I do 'have machine, will travel.'" In retrospect, I admit it may have looked more like an appliance than a sewing machine. That did not, however, discourage me from promptly delivering one of my minilectures on the importance of having one's machine nearby at all times. Since I am a traveling teacher and lecturer, my case is extreme. There are many times when I need a machine for workshops, demonstrations, vacations or servicing.

When I am not traveling, my machine is in my studio. Just the mention of the word *studio* transforms a sewing space into something special. It suggests creative isolation set to your own priorities: phone close by or disconnected, silence or symphony music in the background, soap operas, or continuous weather on TV. Ah, the Perfect Patchwork Day: beds somewhat straightened—not made; meals organized—not finished; mail answered—just the bills; laundry done—never put away; then a race to the studio. You might employ the "dangling carrot." Time spent in your studio becomes a reward for attending to those mundane household activities. You have to be very particular about domestic disregard.

## STUDIO PLANNING

Have you examined your sewing setup lately? Do you want to create a more inviting, comfortable sewing studio? Check your floor plan. The three essential parts of your studio should revolve around a triangular arrangement of a cutting and drafting space, a pressing area, and a sewing area.

**The cutting and drafting space** should have books, magazines, and other inspirational literature at your fingertips, and fabric positioned nearby. Just mentioning fabric gets the juices

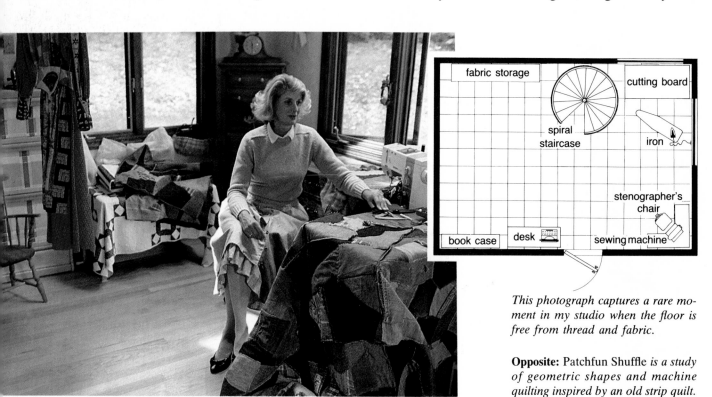

*This photograph captures a rare moment in my studio when the floor is free from thread and fabric.*

**Opposite:** Patchfun Shuffle *is a study of geometric shapes and machine quilting inspired by an old strip quilt.*

flowing. Can you bear to walk through a fabric store and not touch? We are fortunate to have such an array of colors and prints available to us. How do you store your fabric? Stacking and layering fabric on open shelves according to colors allows it to be easily seen. Even remnants need to be seen and separated by colors. All new fabric should be preshrunk, even fabric bought long ago and hidden away.

Other items to include in this area of your studio are a cutting board, drafting board, rulers, pencils, graph paper, tracing pads, mat board, rotary cutter, and scissors.

**The pressing area** needs to be an uncluttered space with plenty of elbow room. It is handy to have the ironing board close to the sewing machine. Keep the board well padded and make sure the height is comfortable. A small, portable board easily accommodates piecework, and the larger standing board handles garments and quilt tops. If you are sewing many garments, look into other padded notions, such as a seam roll, a needle board for napped fabrics, a pressing mitt, or a tailor's ham. A standard iron for home use and a travel iron for the road are necessities. Keep the surface of the iron clean and use only the prescribed type of water for steaming.

**The sewing area** of your studio is obviously dominated by your sewing machine. Today, the sewing machine is not just a utilitarian mechanism used for garments and curtains. It is also a tool involved in the creative process. Did you know that, except for the clock, the sewing machine was the first industrially produced domestic machine? It even predates the vacuum cleaner. No wonder exciting, crafty, innovative people have dirty houses! They know creative clutter is better than idle neatness.

*Dark sashing highlights the many sampler blocks in* **Shirley's Sampler.**

*SEWING MACHINE UPDATE*

Where is your machine positioned? If you have to plunk your machine on the kitchen table and rush through a project in order to make way for dinner, rethink your plan. Isn't there a corner in the bedroom, hall area, or even the dining room that could be screened off when not in use? The machine should be available at all times, not hidden in a case.

Have you considered using a stenographer's chair while working at the sewing machine? You can adjust the seat height—20 inches is right for me. The wheels allow you to easily scoot to the iron. No matter what chair you sit in, you should be able to look down on the throat plate and the needle. You should not have to reach up towards that area of your sewing machine.

How well do you know your machine? Become familiar with the terminology of all its parts. Then when you call the repairman, you won't have to refer to a part as the "thing-a-mabob" or "whatcha-ma-call-it." Can you update your present machine? Read your manual thoroughly and keep it close to the sewing area. If you are entitled to private instructions with the purchase of your machine, take full advantage of them.

**Hints for Caring for Your Sewing Machine**
- Keep your machine covered when not in use.
- Use a thread of good quality; inexpensive thread hinders the mechanism.
- Keep plenty of bobbins loaded; check plastic bobbins for any irregularities.
- Oil your machine; follow the guidelines in your maintenance book.
- Keep the area around the feed dogs and bobbin case free of lint; the spray cans of air sold in photography stores are ideal for cleaning away lint.
- Always turn the handwheel towards you; do not push or turn it in a backward motion.

Become familiar with the most popular presser feet available for your machine. Even if you have had a tendency to shy away from that box of intricate devices, remember that taking the time to explore them might open up new sewing avenues.

The most important part of the sewing machine is the needle. When you are sewing frequently, needles need to be replaced often. Don't tug on the needle when you snip your threads. Angle your threads away from the presser foot before you snip. This will prevent you from bending or breaking your needle. (You might want to save your old needles; they make great nails when you are hanging lightweight objects on the wall.)

### THE LATEST IN NOTIONS

Ready? You won't be completely ready until you have investigated the wonderful array of quilt and sewing notions available today. Precision piecing can only be accomplished with the proper tools. The perfect straight line, the precise cut, and the exact 45° angle all combine to create your ultimate goal—the warm and beautiful quilt. Notions are continually updated, but learn to use what is available now. Discover drafting stores that sell a wonder of precision instruments.

**Try to Keep on Hand**
- Cutting tools
Heavy scissors for cutting layers (have some sort of identifying mark on these to guard against workshop bandits)
Lightweight scissors, for frequent cutting
Embroidery scissors, for buttonholes and precision cutting in other tight areas
Appliqué trimmers
Clippers
Rotary cutter and mat
- Fold-out cutting board

- Rulers—thick and thin
- Right angles
- Compass
- Templates—translucent plastic
- Marking devices—pencils, white chalk markers, water-erasable pens
- Pencil sharpener
- Tracing paper
- Graph paper—check to see that the graph is "true"
- Quilter's quarters—a plastic ¼″ cube, 8″ in length
- Bias bars
- Bias makers
- Quilting needles and pins
- Magnetic pincushion
- Masking tape
- Point turner
- Batting—a variety of types
- Hoops
- Embroidery floss
- Thimbles
- Thread—sewing and quilting

The list of quilting notions may appear overwhelming at first, but you will not need to purchase every item immediately. As your quilting develops, so will your inventory of tools and notions. In fact, as an on-the-go quilter, you may eventually find yourself struggling under a mountain of paraphernalia, trying to balance all the gadgets of the craft in your coat pockets and purse. Taking time to make yourself this handy tote may be the answer.

### THE ULTIMATE TOTE
(photograph on page 83)

This satchel is designed with two large compartments, each open at one end. One compartment holds the cutting mat and the other holds a lap board. The compartments are secured across the base or spine with an open-ended pocket for rulers. Notions are stored inside the many other pockets.

## Materials

2 yards of double-faced prequilted fabric
1 yard of wide webbing for handles
Pockets from old blue jeans
8 yards of bias tape
Large buttons or Velcro

## Method

Cut the fabric into two rectangles, each measuring 27″ x 44″. Cut the webbing into two 10″ lengths and two 8″ lengths.

Fold the rectangle used for the inside of the tote in half to find the center line. From the center line, measure 2″ to each side and mark these lines as stitching lines. Within this 4″ area, sew elastic and ribbons to hold your spools of thread. (Figure 1.) Position the pockets so that they will be upright when you are carrying your tote. Attach your pockets with a zigzag stitch so that you don't have to turn under any edges.

Center the two 10″ handles on each end of the rectangle, with handle ends 6″ apart. Bind all four edges of the rectangle with bias tape.

Find the center of the outside rectangle. Measure 2″ to each side and mark stitching lines. Sew on any large pockets for carrying books. Attach two 8″ handles with ends 4″ apart. (Figure 2.) Bind all the raw edges with bias tape.

Align the two rectangles with wrong sides together. Machine-stitch through both rectangles following the stitching lines. The open space between the two lines becomes a pocket, open at each end, for your large ruler. Using a zipper foot, sew the sides of both rectangles together, stitching inside the bias tape. Leave the pocket for the ruler open.

Buttons or Velcro will secure the wide top opening. Load your tote with quilting supplies; slip the shorter handles through the longer handles; and you are ready to go. (Figure 3.)

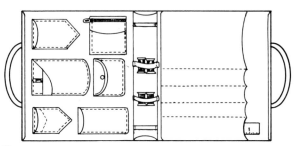
Figure 1

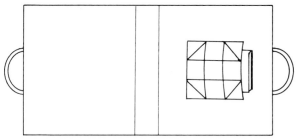
Figure 2

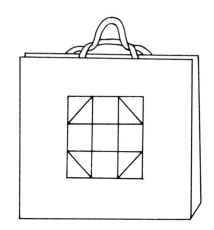
Figure 3

## SELECTING FABRICS

Before the first stitch on your quilt can be taken you must decide on your design and fabric. Since you will live with your choice of color for a long time, think it through carefully. The many photographs of finished quilts in this book are meant to inspire you and to trigger your imagination. Even if the same fabric and design are chosen by many quilters, each quilt will become one of a kind, for the hands of every quilter will apply their own unique touch.

Check your hoard of fabrics. This may be a great source of inspiration. I have found that 100% cotton fabric responds best to small piecework, but I do not rule out using blends. If a fabric's composition is unknown, you might try the burn test to determine if polyester is present. (A "burn test" means just what it says. Burn a small scrap of the fabric. Cotton has a slow, even burn and leaves a fine ash; cotton/polyester burns quickly and gives off black smoke, leaving a dark crust.) Keep velvets, corduroy, and nap fabrics for novelty projects.

Always buy extra material to allow for mistakes or a change of mind. The design that looks fine on paper may need altering once piecing is started. Remember, if you are making a border out of a solid piece of fabric, rather than piecing a border, you will need to purchase fabric the length of your quilt. Large remnants left over from cutting the pieces for the quilt blocks can be used for pieced borders.

### DRAFTING YOUR OWN DESIGN

Although there are many new sampler blocks introduced in *More Lap Quilting*, you may find designing your own block rewarding. Do not be afraid to tackle this part of the quilting process. Just being a quilter puts you in touch with the enormous possibility of potential designs you see around you every day. A chance observation of a picture in a gift shop inspired my Shadow Dance design, and I first saw the Variable Star pattern on steps leading to a quaint row house in London. The simple steps I followed in adapting the star design to a quilting pattern might help you in creating or adapting your block designs.

- Decide on the division within the basic block. Is the pattern a natural four-patch or nine-patch, an asymmetrical or diagonal pattern, or a design best adapted to appliqué?
- Use graph paper to plot your design. Experiment with colored pencils for various alternatives until you find the most effective design combination. (Figure 4.)
- Enlarge the design to make an exact copy of the quilt block. Decide which templates will be needed. Add ¼″ seam allowances to the templates, and mark the grain lines so that no bias edges are on the outside of the block. Cut a set of trial patterns from fabric and experiment with the construction of the block.

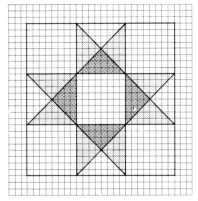 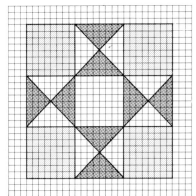 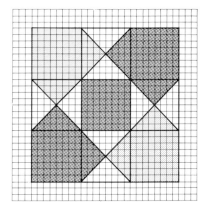

Figure 4

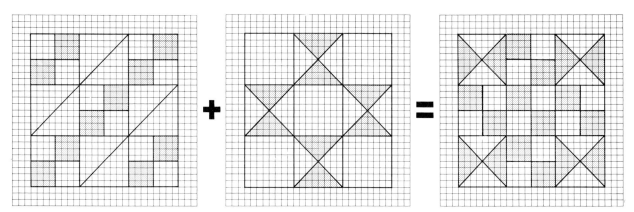

Figure 5

If drafting your own designs does not appeal to you, there are other ways to add originality to your quilts. Consider combining two previously popular patterns into a new design, as I have done in Buttons and Bows for the quilt *Gypsy in My Soul*. There is practically no limit to the design possibilities. After you have drawn your blocks, cut out the different segments and rearrange them. You will be amazed at the outcome. (Figure 5.)

### TRANSFERRING TEMPLATES

Proper template transfer from book to plastic or cardboard is essential. An alternative to plastic templates are templates made from cardboard and covered with transparent Con-Tact paper. Paper templates will rip and just do not last. The templates for all the quilts in this book include a grain line and a 1/4" seam allowance. The grain line may align with the crosswise or the straight of grain.

To transfer the template from the book, use a piece of sturdy plastic and an indelible pen. As you trace each pattern, mark the grain lines, the outside cutting edge, and the 1/4" seam allowance onto the plastic. Label the right side of each template. Punch out the turns with a small 1/8" hole punch. (Figure 6.)

In preparation for template transfer, preshrink all fabric, and press it while it is still damp.

Position the template on the fabric, noting how the pattern of fabric falls within the boundaries of the seam lines. Using a water-erasable pen, pencil, or a thin sliver of soap, trace around the template and cut out the fabric shape. Turn the fabric piece wrong side up and mark all corner turns indicated by the holes in the template.

I have found that a lapboard, with fine sandpaper attached to the top, is an ideal work surface. The sandpaper prevents annoying fabric slippage, and this portable unit can be used in front of the TV or wherever you choose.

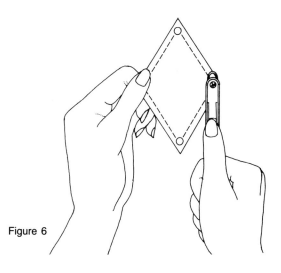

Figure 6

## USING THE ROTARY CUTTER

Although scissors are our mainstay—and where would patchwork be without them?—consider the rotary cutter. The rotary cutter provides a precise cut and the advantage of cutting up to eight layers of fabric at one time. Working with a clear thick quilter's ruler, a rotary cutter, and a companion mat board allows you to see and cut many consecutive layers. Several small pieces of self-adhesive sandpaper on the underside of the ruler will help prevent the ruler from sliding over the fabric while you are cutting long sections. Try to position the mat board so that you have access to all sides of it while cutting out your fabric. (Figure 7.)

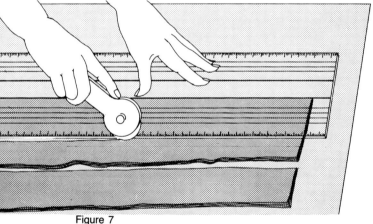

Figure 7

The rotary cutter and mat can also be used for cutting out geometric shapes. The secret is using a see-through, right-angle triangle that has a thick edge. The triangle is less cumbersome than a large ruler when you are working with small shapes. Match the grain lines of the template and fabric and then position the triangle on top. Use the rotary cutter with the blade against the edge of the triangle. With some shapes, such as parallelograms or trapezoids, you must layer the fabric with all the right sides up to ensure that the pieces are uniform. With other shapes, such as squares or diamonds, you can layer fabric back to back or front to front.

## PIECING

A picture of the finished block kept close by will certainly facilitate this next step. Whether sewing by hand or machine, the same ¼″ seam allowance is used. If you choose to piece your block by hand, be sure you have a proper knot in a single strand of thread. (Quilting thread provides additional strength.) Align the pieces with the right sides and raw edges together and pin in place. Take two or three stitches, or as many stitches as possible, before pulling the needle through the fabric. Each time you insert the needle again, take a backstitch to lock your stitches. End each seam with a double-loop knot. Your stitching should stop at the ¼″ turn.

Patchwork can be the perfect place to practice your machine stitching, since you will be sewing many short, straight lines. I recommend a moderate speed and a visual point of control, whether it's the needle, masking tape on the throat plate, or a marked seam allowance. It takes a keen eye to navigate a repeated motion. (It isn't necessary to backstitch when machine piecing if the seams cross.)

Curved piecing on the machine can be achieved with practice and patience. When machine piecing blocks like Virginia's Choice and Drunkard's Path, hold the concave piece against the throat plate and gently swing the convex raw edge around to meet it, stitching on the seam line. Pinning the midpoint before sewing will help you be on target as you make the swing. (Figures 8, 9, 10.)

Machine piecing the inside right angle of a point, such as the 90° angles on the star, also requires close attention. Carefully sew up to the ¼″ turn (point A); stop and backstitch. This allows the seam to be free floating. Align the other side of the corner square, right sides together, with the next star point. Sew from point A to the outside edge. (Figure 11.)

When piecing blocks together, it is best to begin by joining the smallest pieces first. Then join these units to form a completed block.

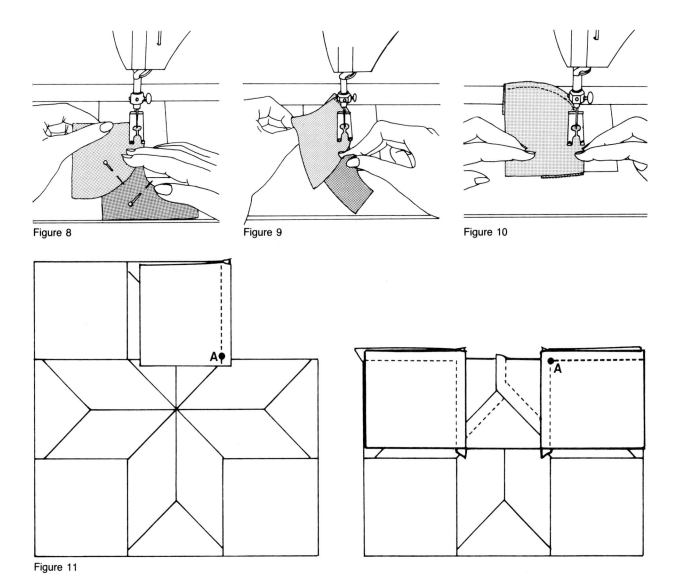

Figure 8

Figure 9

Figure 10

Figure 11

(The broken lines that extend from the blocks in Chapter 10 show you how I pieced each block together.)

Frequent trips to the ironing board while piecing and the use of a master template will guarantee uniformity of block sections before final block assembly. A master template is a template equal to the finished size of your assembled pieces. For example, if you begin piecing by attaching two T37 triangles to form a 3″-square, template S4 can be used as a master template to check your pieced section for accuracy. As you piece your block, compare each small section to a master template.

If the completed section has shrunk before your very eyes, check to see if the seam allowances are too large, the templates are incorrect, or the fabric sections are cut too small.

By the same token, an oversized block may be the result of seam allowances that are too small, incorrect templates, or fabric pieces cut too large. Constant checking with the master template as the block is in progress will help you avoid using the seam ripper. The use of the seam ripper, however, is not a catastrophe. I believe that it builds character and cautions you against making the same mistake twice—at least this is the theory.

Now, take a deep breath and correct any mistakes you might discover; it will save considerable aggravation later. Enjoy your patchwork while anticipating your next step—the actual quilting.

# Lap Quilting Update

Lap quilting, quilt-as-you-go, sectional quilting, apartment quilting, the portable quilt—all these terms refer to a convenient method of quilt construction. The idea is to develop blocks that are quilted individually and then sewn together to build an entire quilt. Some of my recent designs, however, call for a large pieced center section or center panel, as in *Spinning Spools* and *Gypsy in My Soul*, to be quilted using a portable hoop. Whether you are quilting individual blocks or interior panels, each step in the lap-quilting process has its rewards and is dependent on the other steps for its success.

The lap-quilting process really begins once all the blocks are pieced. Remove any remaining fabric markings with a clean damp sponge, and press seams in the direction they have been sewn. Also press the right side of the block. Remove any remaining dog ears and threads.

Check for true right angles and ample ¼″ seam allowances around the perimeter of each block. To do this, lay a "master block" on the reverse side of each pieced block. The master block is a template cut to the exact size of your block minus the ¼″ seam allowance. (The master templates discussed in Chapter 1 are smaller templates the size of a small pieced section within the block.) Trace around the master block with a pencil, leaving your ¼″ seam allowance on the outside. This outline becomes the guide for attaching borders or making block-to-block connections.

### BORDERS AND SETTINGS

The addition of borders to your quilt blocks can greatly alter the look and size of a quilt. One of the most popular borders used is the mitered border. Mitered borders frame blocks with diagonal seams at each corner. (Figure 1.)

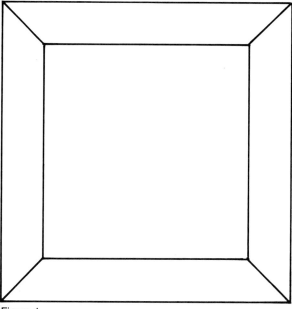

Figure 1

Decide on the width of the mitered border. The length of the border is equal to *twice* the width (including seam allowances) plus the width of the block. An easy formula to follow:

2 x width of border (including seam allowances)
+ width of block
= length of border

For example, a 3″-wide border has the following measurements:

2 x 3½″ (½″ for seam allowances)
= 7″ + 12″ (width of block)
= 19″

Cut your four border strips 3½″ x 19″. If you are planning a double mitered border, sew the two fabrics together in a long band before cutting the four borders. Cut all borders on the straight of grain, since crosswise grain tends to have more give at the corners.

## Perfect Mitering

Cut four borders. Align the right side of one border with the right side of the block, so that equal amounts of the border strip extend from each end of the block. Begin sewing ¼" in from the raw edge of the block, following the previously marked seam line. Backstitch to the seam line and stitch to other end, stopping at the opposite seam line; backstitch to secure. Continue to add the other three borders in the same way. Notice the loose right angle that occurs at each corner. (Figure 2.)

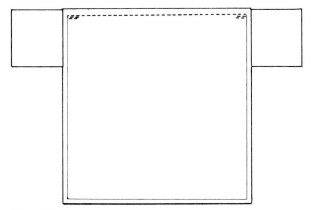

Figure 2

Turn the block and attached borders right side up. Trim the border extensions, using the adjacent border's raw edge as a guide. This forms an overlapping right angle at each of the four corners. (Figure 3.)

Align the border extensions with right sides facing one another and corners square. Holding the seam allowance, draw a straight diagonal line from the backstitching point to the outside corner. This becomes your stitching guide. Start sewing at the backstitching, and continue sewing following your guideline. Trim excess fabric, leaving a ¼" seam allowance. (Figure 4.) Press diagonal mitered seams in same direction

at each corner. The seams between the blocks and border are pressed in the same direction, either toward the block if quilting on the border or away from the block if quilting on edge of block. Save all those leftover triangles for your next quilt.

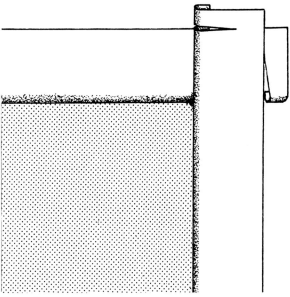

Figure 3

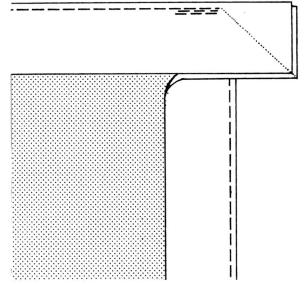

Figure 4

Mitered borders and their variations can bring a great deal of originality to the look of your finished quilt. Attaching blocks with mitered borders directly to one another creates a frame for your block design, as seen in *Mexican Star*. (Figure 5.)

Varying the typical mitered border by using two light and two dark borders on opposite sides creates the spinning effect seen in the large sampler blocks in the quilt *Spinning Spools*. (Figure 6.)

Inserting a 1″-wide dark accent strip before attaching a mitered border accentuates each of the blocks surrounding the center panel in *Gypsy in My Soul*. (Figure 7.)

In addition to mitered borders, other borders and settings can add new life to the traditional quilt. Some of those used for the quilts in this book are shown on the opposite page. Drafting your borders and setting on graph paper helps you to visualize the possibilities.

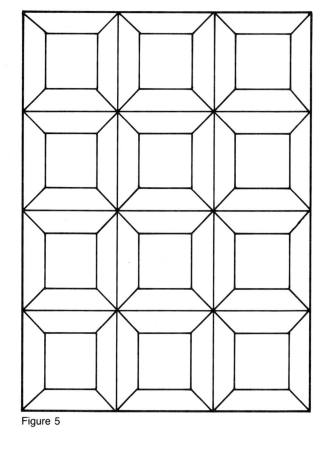

Figure 5

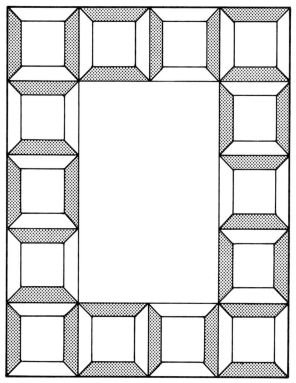

Figure 6

Figure 7

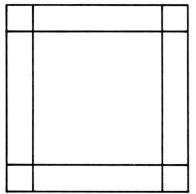

Figure 8

*Corner inserts with a single band are seen in* Stars Over the Smokies *in Chapter 6. In this instance, strips are added to opposite sides first. Corner inserts are then sewn to both ends of each of the other two border strips. These two pieced border strips are then pinned and aligned with the attached border before being sewn in place. Sometimes elaborate corner inserts can be pieced into a small block.*

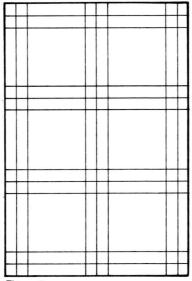

Figure 9

*Joining blocks that have a single border and border inserts creates the look of a double border. Borders are added to the perimeter of the quilt for balance.*

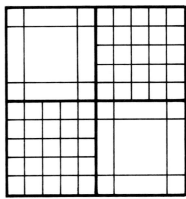

Figure 10

*There are times when borders would interfere with the quilt design. In the quilt* Double Irish Chain, *the blocks are attached without additional borders. Four blocks are attached together to form one unit. When these units are attached to one another, an unbroken, overall design is created.*

Figure 11

*In the* String Along Lily *quilt in Chapter 8, the borderless blocks are set together on the diagonal.*

Figure 12

*A variation of the diagonal setting was used in the quilt* Rescue the Perishing, *in Chapter 4. Triangles act as the blocks' borders. These blocks are first put together in strips for row lap quilting; then the strips are offset when they are attached to one another. This forms an unusual zigzag pattern.*

## THE QUILTING PROCESS

Once you have decided on your borders and the overall quilt setting, it's time to plan your quilting lines—time to put the icing on the cake. Quilting enhances your patchwork design. It is better if you decide and mark where the quilting is to be before batting, backing, and block are basted together, because it is easier to mark a flat, pieced surface than a basted layer. If masking tape—best for straight-line quilting—or Con-Tact paper stencils are used, you can eliminate this step and start the temporary basting of layers together.

Quilting designs are given for many of the pieced blocks in this book, but they are merely suggestions. To decide on your quilting pattern, evaluate your block. Does it have direction? Do you want to emphasize star points? What is the overall feeling? The most traditional form of quilting is outline quilting, which emphasizes the piecework with the quilting lines stitched ¼″ or ⅛″ from the pieced seams. However, original quilting designs can set your quilt apart and make it truly your own.

A new quilting trend is to have quilting lines that contrast with the block design. For example, use a fan design on top of a log cabin square or a feather wreath with the star pattern. Be creative, but remember that lap-quilting blocks must have at least ½″ free on all outside edges for block and row assembly. This ½″ will accommodate the ¼″ seam allowance needed when you join your blocks.

### Transferring Stencils

The method of stencil transfer can be varied depending upon your supplies. Pencils, soap slivers, water-erasable pens, or soapstone markers are all possibilities. If the stencil design is on paper (copied from a book), try taping it to a sunny window and placing the cloth on top for marking. A glass-topped table with a light underneath works equally well. Also popular today are precut stencils or stencils that you make yourself from plastic. These are long wearing, and since they are clear, you can see through to the fabric for easy placement.

### Basting

The completed block, with or without borders, is the pattern for cutting out backing and batting. There are many different types of batting available today. Polyester batting can be fluffy or flat and compact. There is also a thin, flat Pellon fleece batting in combinations of cotton and polyester or varieties of wool. Invest in a good-quality batting to ensure the longevity of your quilt and handiwork. Before cutting out the backings, take into account that the tops already have a ¼″ seam allowance included to accommodate the final assembly. The backings, therefore, do not need to be larger than the pieced blocks.

Since you do not want these three layers—block, batting, backing—to shift while you are quilting, it is necessary at this point to baste them together. Basting is an important step, regardless of the manner in which you quilt. Insufficient basting will cause the layers to shift, creating tucks and irregularities in the backing as you quilt. Align all corners, pin in place, and using a contrasting thread, take long basting stitches that can easily be removed later. Start in the center and work out.

### Quilting

The actual quilting process is the connecting of the three layers with tiny quilting stitches. Many quilters find quilting the most rewarding and relaxing time spent with their project. Whether it is by hand or by machine, the quilting adds an all-important third dimension to your work by creating subtle shadows and nuances of depth that highlight the piecework. Two distinct forms of quilting, hand quilting and machine quilting, serve varying needs and accommodate a multitude of quilting requirements. Only by trial and error can you discover the technique best suited to you.

### Hand Quilting

Hand quilting can refer to all of these: free-hand stitching without a hoop or frame; hand stitching within a portable hoop or frame that permits turning the item being stitched for easy access; or hand stitching on a quilt that is attached to a large, standing quilting frame. Each of these hand-quilting methods has its own peculiarities; however, certain basic needle and thread techniques apply.

With all forms of quilting, a hidden knot is essential, and the fewer knots in any quilt the better. You can eliminate a knot when starting by using a double length of quilting thread, about 30″ long. Pull only 15″ of the thread through; quilt that length out, and then return to the 15″ that was left dangling and quilt that out. When you reach the ends of the thread, form a knot by making a loop with the thread. Use the point of the needle to keep the knot close to the fabric as the thread is pulled tight. Take a half backstitch, bringing up the needle about an inch away. Tug the knot through the front, leaving the knot hidden in the layer of batting. Clip the dangling thread end. (Sometimes a dangling thread is left on the outside edge of the block, to be picked up and used for quilting after the blocks are assembled.)

**The foolproof knot** is used when you prefer to begin quilting with a knotted thread, and you want to hide the knot in the batting before taking any stitches. To make a foolproof knot, thread the needle with 12″ to 18″ of thread. Draw the thread into a circle and hold with the eye of the needle between your right thumb and forefinger. (Figure 13.)

Wrap the thread around the needle two or three times with your left hand. Slide this coil of thread down the needle until you can hold it, along with the eye and the thread end, in your right hand. (Figure 14.)

Holding the eye of the needle with your left hand, slide the coil down the thread until it tightens. (Figure 15.) Trim any tail off the end. After a little practice, you will have a perfect knot every time.

For open, loosely woven fabric, try wrapping the thread around the needle three or four times. For tightly woven fabric, just one or two wraps will do.

**Now for the quilting:** Always start your quilting in the center of the basted block to prevent the fabric from puckering. Hand quilting without a frame or hoop requires a running stitch. The needle enters the layers at an angle, while the fingers of the "off hand" ensure that

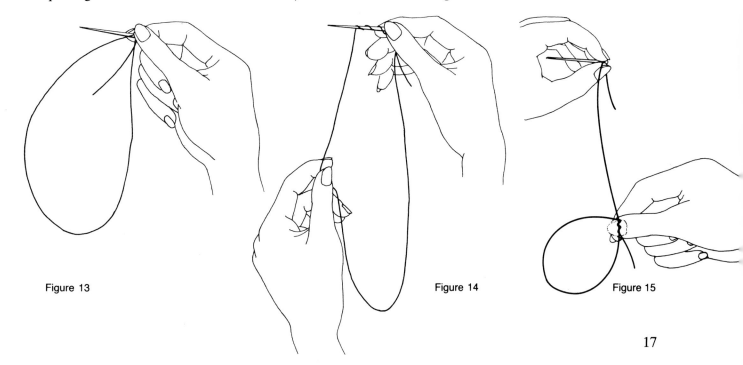

Figure 13                    Figure 14          Figure 15

17

all three layers are caught in each stitch. In this method of quilting, the bottom stitches can become slightly displaced. I would encourage you to use a thimble and something to protect the off finger that is acting as a guide underneath the block. Students have devised many strange ways to save the quilt from blood stains created by unsuspecting fingers injured in the line of duty.

When working with a portable frame or hoop, another stitch approach is necessary. I call this the "rocking" method, with the eye of the needle steered by the tip of the thimble. (An indented thimble is ideal for the job.) The thumb is out in front to balance the up-and-down rocking motion, while underneath, the other hand works with the thumb to free the material. This method produces bottom stitches that line up with the top stitches in a consistent manner. Using a portable frame or hoop allows you to turn your work around, offering easy accessibility to all sides.

With the traditional standing frame, you quilt in two directions (unless you are ambidextrous) with a similar rocking motion. This takes some preplanning. Dangling threads that can be picked up to quilt in the opposite direction work well here, since it is most difficult to quilt while standing on one's head! Moving to the opposite side of the frame is an alternative way to get a new quilting angle.

Naturally we all take pride in our small, consistent stitches, but that one uneven stitch in a row of otherwise perfect stitches imparts the warmth of the human touch.

**Machine Quilting**

Machine quilting has opened up many exciting new vistas for the innovative quilter. Basting is just as important for machine work as for hand quilting, but be careful not to catch your basting stitches in the presser foot. When you select your thread color, remember that the top thread and the bobbin thread can be the same color, or the bobbin thread can match the color

of the backing. Never use quilting thread in the machine; it will not work. You might consider a monofilament thread or a variegated thread. A zipper foot allows you to confine the machine stitching to the seams of the piecework; this technique, known as quilting "in the ditch," is a very effective approach to quilting if you do not want stitching lines to spoil the look of your piecework.

Another form of machine quilting is done with a wide zigzag stitch sewn directly on top of the pieced seam, either through all three layers or just through the top and batting. This technique can be seen in *Stacking Spools Baby Quilt,* in Chapter 4. This quilt is also an example of quilting in the ditch.

Using a hoop for machine quilting is optional. A thin hoop does stabilize the work; keep the larger hoop on the bottom and insert the smaller hoop on the top of the fabric. If you are quilting with the feed dogs up, the hoop must be moved as you progress. If the feed dogs are dropped, I find the hoop a necessity. This freewheeling form of quilting on the machine is sometimes called "loitering," "meandering," or "free motion."

The writing on the quilt, *Patchfun Shuffle,* shown in Chapter 5 was done on the machine, starting in the center of each panel. I first wrote the script with a fabric marker to provide a guide; then I dropped the feed dogs, attached a darning foot, and using a hoop, machine-stitched my messages. I removed excess basting threads once the hoop was positioned.

Machine quilting like this does take concentration and some practice, but there is a flow of energy that rushes from mind to needle that is most exciting! Another machine quilting technique called "thread sketching" calls for a particular design to be filled in with continuous straight or zigzag stitches. (I've found that my best machine quilting is done in the morning rather than after a full day's work.)

## ASSEMBLING YOUR QUILT

After many enjoyable hours of quilting, the assembly of your quilt can begin. Clean up the blocks by removing all the basting threads, masking tape, and any fabric marker lines. Trim all sides of the blocks so that the block, batting, and backing are even. Working on a clean floor or a bed, arrange the blocks and establish rows that can be connected, either horizontally or vertically. To help you remember your arrangement, label each block's position with a fabric marker or draw a simple diagram on paper.

Whether your blocks are bordered or set together in four-block units, you will attach your blocks to form rows and then attach these rows to form the quilt.

### Block-to-Block Assembly

1. Select two adjacent blocks and lay them on a flat surface with the backing side up. Pin the backing and batting away from the seam to be sewn, revealing the raw edges of the front of the block.

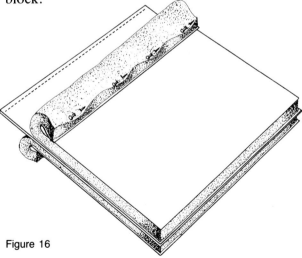

Figure 16

2. Pin the fronts of two blocks together at the corners and in the center, easing where necessary. Machine-stitch, leaving a ¼″ seam allowance. (Figure 16.) You may release one side of the batting and include it in the seam at this time, but remember to keep the batting against

the feed dogs to prevent it from being caught in the needle. (Figure 17.)

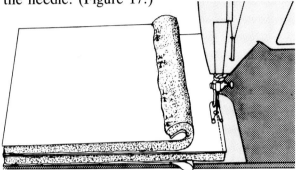

Figure 17

3. Continue to sew the blocks together in this way until the row is complete. Thumb-crease the seams closed and all in one direction. Alternate the direction of the creased seam from one row to the next.

4. Lay the row of assembled blocks with the backing side up. Unpin the backing and batting. Trim the batting in the attached blocks so that it butts up against the adjacent batting but does not overlap it.

5. Smooth the backing of one of the blocks over the seam and batting. Turn under the other backing ¼″ and slip-stitch this flat lapped seam in place with coordinating thread. (Figure 18.)

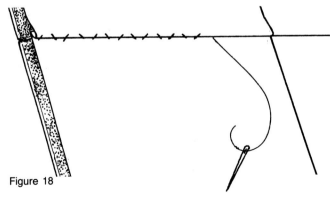

Figure 18

This entire block-to-block assembly process can be reversed. The backings may be machine-stitched together and the seams on the front of the quilt slip-stitched into place. This is the procedure I followed with the *Gypsy in My Soul* quilt. (See Chapter 4.)

19

### Row-to-Row Assembly

Once the blocks are connected in rows, you can begin the row-to-row assembly. This will take a lot of space, so you may want to set up your machine on a large surface such as a dining room table. If at some point during this next step you become discouraged, just remember,

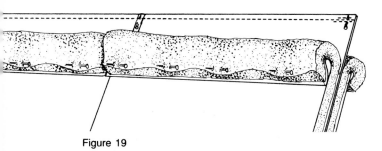

Figure 19

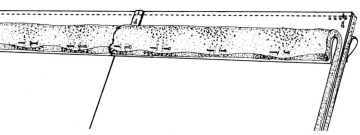

Figure 20

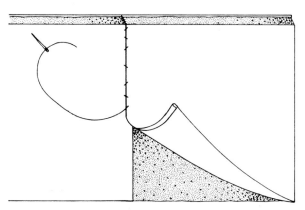

Figure 21

the quilting is all done and this is the last leg of the journey. Two methods of row-to-row assembly are described here.

### Method 1

This method is exactly the same as block-to-block assembly. Pin the backing and unattached batting of the assembled blocks away from the fronts. Align the intersections of each row and secure with pins. (Basting will help to ease fabric between intersections.) Machine-stitch the rows together with a ¼″ seam. (Figure 19.) One side of the batting could be released and included in the seam if you desire. (Figure 20.) Backstitch at each end of the row.

Spread out the connected rows on a large flat surface with the backing side up. Trim the batting, so it just butts together. Smooth the backing of one row over the seam and batting. Turn under the backing of the other row ¼″, pin or baste, and slip-stitch by hand. Be careful not to take stitches through the quilt top during this step. (Figure 21.)

### Method 2

If you are using a lightweight batting, you can choose to connect five layers, as opposed to two or three layers as described in Method 1. Baste these five layers (backing, batting, top, top, batting), carefully aligning the intersections of your rows. Machine-stitch the five layers together. Turn the only remaining layer, the unattached backing, under ¼″ and slip-stitch into place.

After your whole quilt is assembled, you may find areas that you wanted to quilt before, but were unable to do so because they were too close to a seam. With the aid of a portable hoop, you can quilt along the edges of your blocks before or after the folded lap of the backing is stitched into place.

**Opposite:** *From the cover of my first book,* Lap Quilting, *to quilted wall hanging! The impact of strong colors sets off* Star Bright.

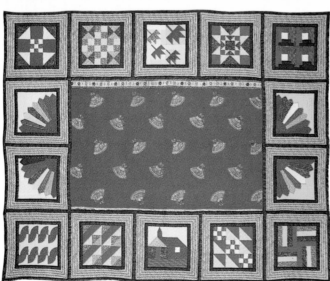

*The vibrant colors and spirit of the quilt,* Gypsy in My Soul, *just match this award-winning 1911 Maxwell car. (I saved the triangles from many mitered corners to make a border for my apron.)*

*Waste not, want not! Many shades of red, pink, and maroon string-pieced diamonds stand out in a field of white in* String Along Lily.

*Sampler blocks in* Rescue the Perishing *are arranged on point and float on a field of dark calico. The zigzag design, created by staggering the blocks, provides a new setting for old friends.*

*Fall in love with appliqué and the
many combinations of floral and
heart designs in this nine-block quilt,*
Romance of the Roses.

*Use remnants from your quilts to frame those special photographs.*

*Baskets of geometric lilies enhance the center of* Lottie's Lily *while a single posy decorates each triangular border section. The design of this antique block was the inspiration for my* Lottie's Lily *block found in* Spinning Spools.

*Pastel remnants form the bricks cascading down the pieced strips that alternate with the pink panels in* Pink Brick Path.

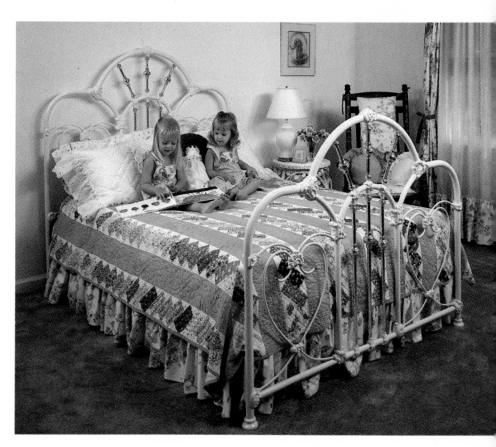

**Opposite:** *Pink tulips are appliquéd in the corners of the 14" blocks of* Tri-State Tulip. *The center section of the quilt is surrounded by borders enhanced by clamshell quilting.*

27

# The Finishing Touch

## BINDINGS AND EDGES

A quilt isn't complete until you add a proper finished edge. There are several considerations at this point. Is the quilt the right size? Will the quilt rest on a larger-sized bed than you had originally intended and therefore need a border? Do you want a novelty addition of ruffles or lace? Consider the style of the quilt. For instance, neither curved piecework nor appliqué lends itself to sharp triangular accents. A key to a successful finish is planning. Plan your finishing touches as carefully as you planned the rest of your quilt.

### Bias Edges

Have you ever wondered why a double-fold bias edge is preferable to a straight-of-the-grain edging for your quilt? It's because the outside edge of a quilt gets a lot of wear and is often the first thing to deteriorate. One thread resting at the edge in a straight-of-the-grain fabric receives so much wear that it will soon fray with use, but diagonal threads from a bias can distribute the wear and tear. A double-fold bias offers even more protection.

Bias binding may be purchased, or you can make your own. Making your own is more economical and allows you to coordinate the binding with the quilt. But sometimes it's hard to figure how much fabric to buy for a continuous bias strip for a finished quilt or pillow ruffle. Each quilt featured in *More Lap Quilting* is accompanied by the perimeter measurement. If you know how wide a bias edging you want and the length or the measurement of the perimeter of your quilt, the following chart will help you to determine the amount of fabric you need for the quilts. It may also be helpful when you're doing other home decorating projects.

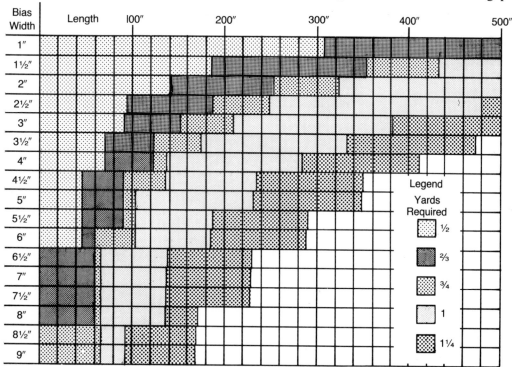

**Opposite:** *One rectangle (R10) is repeated to obtain the staggered brick effect in* Brick Path.

## Making a Continuous Bias Strip

Start with a square piece of fabric. Eliminate the selvage and cut the fabric in half on the diagonal to form two equal triangles. Lay the two triangles, right sides together, so that right angles are at top. (Figure 1.) Machine-stitch with a ¼″ seam allowance. Press seam open. Now the triangles will form a parallelogram. (Figure 2.) Decide how wide you want the bias strip; 2½″ to 3″ is usually appropriate for the outside of a quilt. Mark this measurement with a pencil or fabric marker. (Your finished binding will actually be one-fourth the width of the bias strip.) Make a 6″-long cut down the line you have just marked. Continue to mark across the entire parallelogram to make a guide for cutting. A see-through ruler helps with this step.

Join the right sides of A and B together so that points x and o meet. Sew with a ¼″ seam allowance, joining side A to side B to form a tube. (Figure 3.) Notice that the 6″-long cut extends beyond the side of the tube, and the other side has about the same amount of excess. Use the loose 6″ strip as a starting point and continue cutting the strip around the tube following your lines. Pulling this open tube over the end of an ironing board will help you to avoid snipping the underneath fabric.

## Attaching a Continuous Bias Strip

Hand-baste the outside edges of the quilt together to eliminate any pull of fabric. Straight pins placed at a right angle every inch or so will help to eliminate any pull, but basting is foolproof. Once the bias strip is made, fold it in half with raw edges aligned and gently press. Place the folded bias strip on top of the quilt with the fold toward the inside, and pin in place or baste. Machine-stitch the entire folded bias strip to the quilt top with a ¼″ seam allowance. Corners may be rounded off by gently curving the bias strip at each turn.

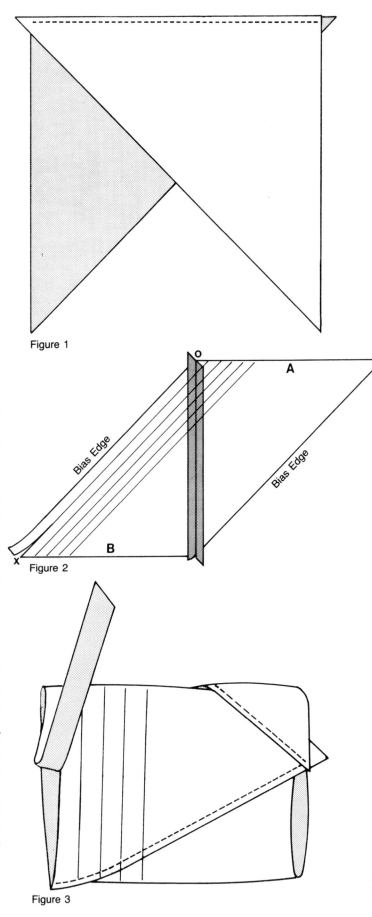

Figure 1

Figure 2

Figure 3

A **perfectly squared-off corner** requires a right angle to be formed with a double bias edging. To do this, use a fabric marker and mark the inside ¼″ turn at each corner of the quilt. Sew the bias strip up to that mark and backstitch. Remove your work from the machine. (Figure 4.)

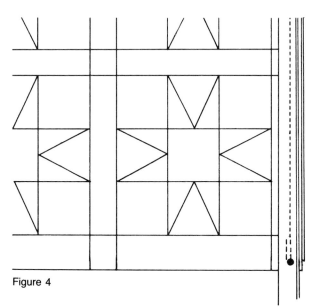

Figure 4

Turn the raw edge of the bias strip at the corner of the quilt and make a ½″ fold. Pinch or pin this together. (Figure 5.)

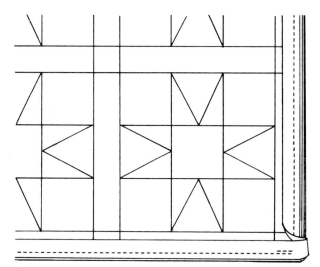

Figure 5

Align the raw edges and machine-stitch perpendicular to the previous backstitching. This will create a perfect diagonal fold on the front and back when the bias strip is folded over. Continue attaching the bias strip to all the raw edges of the quilt.

**A diagonal seam** must be formed where the two ends of the folded bias strip meet. Allow the ends to overlap about 4″. Find the point where the bottom layer of B ends (x) and mark that point on side A. Then find the point where the top layer of side B ends (o) and mark it on side A. (Figure 6.) Unfold side A and mark points ½″ to the right of x and o. Draw a diagonal line between this second set of points and cut along it. (Figure 7.) Once you have cut, you will find you can join the two sides with a perfect ¼″ seam allowance. After sewing A and B together, fold the bias strip in half again and pin or baste it to the quilt.

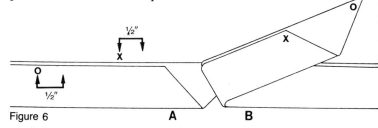

Figure 6          A          B

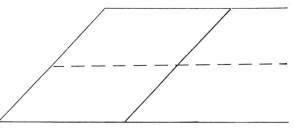

Figure 7

Once you have machine-sewn the bias strip to the quilt top, roll the bias strip over the raw edges and slip-stitch in place just beyond the machine stitching on the back of the quilt. This must be done by hand.

### Rolled Hems

A rolled hem can be used on the front or back of a quilt if each of the perimeter blocks is cut with a 1″ extension on the outside edge. Simply fold the extension to the opposite side of the quilt, turn under ¼″, and then secure it with a slip stitch.

### Self-Finished Edges

Self-finished edges are possible only if the outside edges of the quilt are free of quilting. Trim the batting about ¼″ and turn the raw edges of both the front and back in toward each other. Pin in place and secure with a running stitch. This produces square corners and a nice neat finish.

### Ruffles or Lace

Consider adding a gathered ruffle, eyelet, or even a double ruffle to the border of your quilt. To do this, pin the loose backing away from the batting and front of the quilt. Baste or pin the ruffle or accent to the batting and the front. Machine-sew ¼″ beyond any gathering line. Always have the batting next to the feed dogs and not next to the machine needle. Trim any excess seam allowance; fold seam allowance towards the quilt. Turn backing under ¼″ and slip-stitch in place over the line of machine stitching. A deep ruffle added to your quilt might be an alternative to a separate dust ruffle on your bed.

### The Saw-Toothed Edge

Folded triangles intermesh into a saw-tooth design for a clever accent to many quilt designs. Any size square may be used to form your triangles. (Five-inch squares folded into triangles fit nicely into an 18″ border span.) Fold the squares into triangles and then fold again to form smaller triangles. Interlap the triangles around the perimeter of the quilt. Pin or baste in place and attach as you would a ruffle. Small triangle accents are nice on a baby quilt.

### ADDED BORDERS

Even if you have already quilted your quilt, you can add pieced or plain bands to enlarge it or frame it. Any band or pieced border that is added has to be cut the length of the side before quilting, as there is a certain amount of "take-up" due to quilting. After the border addition is attached, quilting needs to be added for balance. The borders need to work with the design of the entire unit and must not appear to be an afterthought.

The "stack" method is a quick and easy way to attach this addition. With raw edges aligned, stack in the following manner: batting for border; backing of border, right side up; the quilt, right side up; border top, right side down. Baste and machine-stitch these layers together with the batting next to the machine feed dogs. Fold layers outward, baste, quilt, and complete the final raw edge. This process is sometimes called "stack and extend." If all the strips or bands are cut the same width, this is a quick way of making a quilt, because the front and back are made at the same time.

### THE SIGNATURE

Finding a quilt that is personal and appealing is a treat. Discovering a date and initials on it is truly exciting. So take the time to add that final touch for posterity on your own quilt. Either by hand or machine, sign and date your quilt in one corner. This completes the story and highlights all the many steps—and the love—involved in making a quilt.

If there is a personal dedication that you want to display, type the message directly on a piece of muslin. Prepare a cloth frame (see Chapter 9) and insert this muslin fabric inside. Now, stand back and call all your friends to join in this glorious moment of completion.

# Sophisticated Samplers

A fresh, sophisticated approach to the traditionally popular sampler quilt gives you a chance to experiment with new style and flair. In this chapter, you'll explore new ways of setting old familiar patterns and discover some brand new designs. All the necessary information for creating your very own sampler is included for each quilt.

### SPINNING SPOOLS

Small spools, in a lively assortment of fabrics, spin around larger spool sampler blocks that frame a center medallion of even more spools! My interest in this pattern was awakened by a slide of Ruth Roberson's wall hanging, which I had shown many times in my lectures. Ruth created a brilliant red-orange twirl effect in a four-patch rendition of King's X and used string piecing in the trapezoid. Only after many viewings did I see the startling effect of this quilt, aptly named *Tangram Whirl,* suddenly staring me in the face. Four dark offset spools were practically jumping out of the slide.

Tangram Whirl *by Ruth Roberson.*

This design prompted me to research and examine other spool patterns, and eventually inspired my sampler quilt *Spinning Spools.*

In the center panel of *Spinning Spools,* four 12″ spool blocks are joined block-to-block to form a large square, and edged with a narrow band. The four bands vary in color. They are cut 1¼″ x 26½″ and can be either mitered or squared off. The large square is set on point or on the diagonal, and trapezoids are sewn to each side.

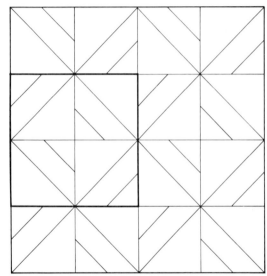

Figure 1

The large spool sampler blocks are formed by attaching 3″-wide mitered borders to a 12″-square block. Alternating colored borders with white borders forms large spools that appear to spin as they move around the center panel.

The angled spools that form the quilt's border are attached to the perimeter blocks before the blocks are quilted so that they may be incorporated in the lap-quilting process. Three angled spools are attached to the outside edge of each perimeter block. A 6″-square section of the spool block is repeated three times to equal 18″. (Figure 1.) Each corner block will be larger than the other blocks because the border sections are attached to the two adjacent sides.

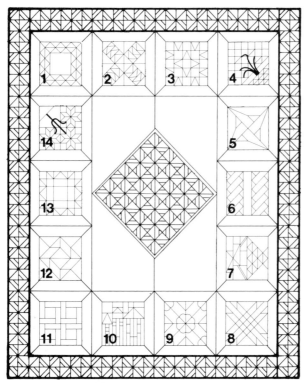

Figure 2. *Spinning Spools*

**Spinning Spools** (photograph on title page)
Finished quilt: 84″ x 102″
Perimeter: 10⅓ yards (372″)
Center panel: 36″ x 54″
Center panel edging: ¾″ wide (cut 1¼″ wide)
Trapezoids: 4 (cut 18½″ x 9¾″ x 25½″ x 27½″)
Sampler blocks: Fourteen 12″-square blocks
(Figure 2)

| | |
|---|---|
| 1. Ocean Waves | 8. Mexican Star |
| 2. Gathering Geese | 9. Virginia's Choice |
| 3. Glow Shine | 10. Rainbow Row |
| 4. Lottie's Lily | 11. Inside Square |
| 5. Shadow Dance | 12. Swirl |
| 6. Brick Walk | 13. Weathervane |
| 7. Bow Basket | 14. Mini Lily |

Mitered borders: 3″ x 18″ (cut 3½″ x 19″)
Outside border: 6″ wide, made up of three 6″
    squares
Fabric requirements: Divide amount needed by
    the number and colors of fabrics used.
    Blocks: 2½ yards
    Borders: 3½ yards
    Center panel: 2 yards
    Backing: 6 yards

## STACKING SPOOLS BABY QUILT

The Spool pattern takes on a new look here. By adding another 6″, or half of the original block, to the 12″-square block, a 12″ x 18″ rectangle is formed. Alternating the colors in the blocks also changes the look. The spool stands out in the blue block, and the pinwheel is more prominent in the yellow block.

Once the blocks are pieced and the borders are attached, cut out the batting the same size as each block. With the batting pinned to the rectangles, machine-quilt. (The backing is added later.)

The blue and yellow blocks are quilted differently. To quilt the yellow blocks, attach a zipper foot to your machine and stitch in the ditch. To quilt the blue blocks, a zigzag stitch is used on the piecing line. Once all the blocks are quilted, sew them together just as you would sew a small nine-patch block.

A double ruffle adds a soft finishing touch. To make the ruffle, cut a 6½″-wide bias strip. Cut another bias strip 2½″ wide out of a different-colored fabric. With right sides together, align the two strips and sew them together along one edge. Turn the fabrics right side out, fold in half, and press. Gather along the raw edge. Ten yards of bias strip are needed for a full ruffle. Baste the ruffle to the right side of the quilt, raw edges aligned.

Place a one-piece backing over the quilt; the ruffle is "sandwiched" between the top and the backing. Sew around entire quilt leaving a 10″ opening. Invert your quilt and hand-stitch the opening. Tie the quilt with tiny yellow ribbons. Tack the ribbon in place, make a bow, and then secure it by machine.

For baby quilts, the priorities are different from those for full-sized quilts. Baby quilts need to be colorful, strong, washable (repeatedly), and quick and easy to make. Sometimes they even need to be made in secret. As a totally machine-sewn project, *Stacking Spools Baby Quilt* meets all these requirements.

## Stacking Spools Baby Quilt

*(photograph on page 47)*

Finished quilt: 45″ x 63″

Perimeter: 6 yards (216″)

Blocks: Nine 12″ x 18″

Mitered borders: 1½″ wide (for each block, cut two 2″ x 15″ and two 2″ x 21″)

Double ruffle: 3″ wide (cut outside ruffle 4″ wide and inside ruffle 2½″ wide)

Fabric requirements: Divide amount needed by number and colors of fabrics used.

   Blocks: 1½″ yards for each of the two colors (3 yards total)

   Ruffle: 10 yards of bias strip, cut 6½″ wide

   Backing: 2 yards

## *GYPSY IN MY SOUL*

A brief glimpse of a gypsy's caravan wagon outside an antique shop in England was the inspiration for this quilt. The vibrant red, maroon, and gold colors lingered in my mind and haunted my imagination.

When I finally started this quilt during a class demonstration, I wanted to update old friends such as Shoo Fly and Grandmother's Fan. I was also experimenting with the idea of a center panel for the quilt. At the same time, I found myself bartering a quilted vest for a smashing batik print from a friend's fabric collection. All red and gold with a spray of wonderful fans dancing across the fabric—there it was—a center panel for my gypsy quilt!

Having a center panel gives you the opportunity to quilt a large unpieced section of the quilt using a hoop. At the same time, it eliminates some of the connecting work and some of the handwork.

Sew your blocks with the backs together. The seam allowance will be on the front side of the blocks. Apply a narrow navy strip to cover the reversed lap-quilting connection. (See Block-to-Block Assembly, page 19.)

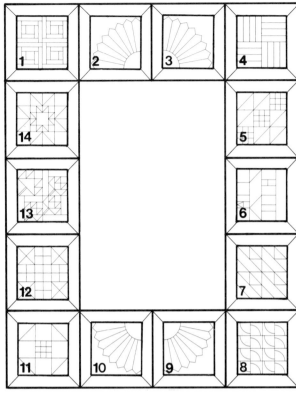

Figure 3. *Gypsy in My Soul*

## *Gypsy in My Soul* (photograph on page 22)

Finished quilt: 80″ x 100″

Perimeter: 10 yards (360″)

Center panel: 40″ x 60″ (cut 40½″ x 60½″)

Sampler blocks: Fourteen 12″ blocks (Figure 3)

| | |
|---|---|
| 1. Log Cabin Four Patch | 8. Drunkard's Path |
| 2. Grandmother's Fan | 9. Grandmother's Fan |
| 3. Grandmother's Fan | 10. Grandmother's Fan |
| 4. Rail Fence | 11. Shoo Fly Variation |
| 5. Nine-Patch Repeat | 12. Buttons & Bows |
| 6. Church on a Hill | 13. Offset Maple Leaf |
| 7. King's X Variation | 14. Double Star Flower |

Narrow borders: 1″ wide (cut 56, 1½″ x 15″)

Mitered borders: 3″ x 20″ (cut 56, 3½″ x 21″)

Fabric requirements: Divide amount needed by number and colors of fabrics used.

   Blocks: 2½ yards

   Panel: 2 yards

   Borders: 3½ yards

   Narrow border: 1 yard

   Backing: 6 yards

## RESCUE THE PERISHING

"Rescue the perishing" pleads the old hymn. My sister rescued a set of ten old square blocks from a church bazaar and sent them to me. I devised an unusual way to incorporate the old blocks into a new design.

Each sampler block is bordered by two large triangles. The large triangles (cut 36) have a right angle and measure 12″ on both sides and 17″ on the diagonal. When making your template, mark the straight of the grain on the diagonal and add a ¼″ seam allowance to all sides. Sew the large border triangles to opposite sides of the sampler blocks to form a parallelogram. (Figure 4.) Sew the parallelograms together to form a row.

Because the rows are staggered, small triangles are needed at the tops and bottoms of certain rows. The small triangles (cut 8) have a right angle and measure 8½″ on the sides and 12″ on the diagonal. The grain line on this triangle is on one of the 8½″ sides, not on the diagonal. The double borders are attached to the rows before the rows are sewn together.

When working with blocks set on point, you need to know the diagonal and right-angle dimensions. To find the diagonal dimension, take the length of the side of the block (12″ in this case), and mul-

Figure 4

tiply it by 1.414. The diagonal for these sampler blocks would equal 16.968 or 17″. Multiplying this figure (17″) by the number of blocks in a row (5) will give you the length of your quilt (85″) before the borders are added. If you are trying to figure the right-angle measurement, multiply the diagonal by .707.

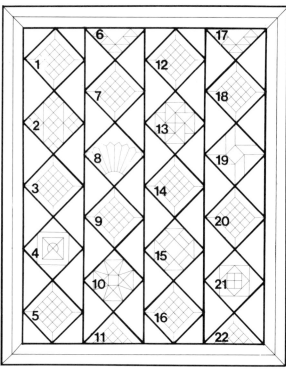

Figure 5. *Rescue the Perishing*

***Rescue the Perishing*** (photograph on page 24)
Finished quilt: 76″ x 93″
Perimeter: 9½ yards (338″)
Sampler blocks: Eighteen 12″ blocks, four half blocks (Figure 5)

1. Rescued Sixteen Patch
2. Jacob's Ladder
3. Rescued Sixteen Patch
4. Mini Moon over the Mountain
5. Rescued Sixteen Patch
6. Saw-toothed Square (half block)
7. Rescued Sixteen Patch
8. Grandmother's Fan
9. Rescued Sixteen Patch
10. Star Daze
11. Rescued Sixteen Patch (half block)
12. Rescued Sixteen Patch
13. Card Tricks
14. Rescued Sixteen Patch
15. Churn Dash
16. Rescued Sixteen Patch
17. Saw-toothed Square (half block)
18. Rescued Sixteen Patch
19. Formal Garden
20. Rescued Sixteen Patch
21. Monkey Wrench
22. Rescued Sixteen Patch (half block)

Fabric requirements: Divide amount needed by the color and number of fabrics used.
Blocks: 3½ yards
Inner border: 9½ yards (cut 2½″ wide)
Outer border: 9¾ yards (cut 2½″ wide)
Backing: 6 yards

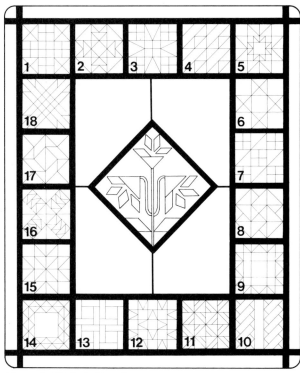

Figure 6. *Shirley's Sampler*

## SHIRLEY'S SAMPLER

Shirley Klennon, a friend and fellow teacher, answered my pleas for another pastel quilt. She was anxious to explore my new designs and offer them to her students. So she created her very own sophisticated sampler, using the String Along Lily motif as the center. Instead of randomly piecing the diamond-shaped petals, Shirley chose a vertical design. She sewed a band of four colors, cut 1″ wide. Then she cut out each diamond with the bands positioned the long, vertical way. She set the lily block on point and used a band to emphasize it. The same dark fabric was used as sashing to separate the sampler blocks. Shirley lap-quilted the sampler blocks in rows. Then the final band was attached using the stack, sew, and extend method.

*Shirley's Sampler* (photograph on page 4)
Finished quilt: 87½″ x 74″
Perimeter: 9 yards (323″)
Center panel: 52½″ x 39″
  Block: 20½″ square (cut 21″)
  Block border: 1½″ x 20½″ (cut 2″ x 21″)
  Pentagon: 9¾″ x 23½″ x 26¼″ x 19½″

Sampler blocks: Eighteen 12″ blocks (Figure 6)

1. Buttons & Bows
2. Double T
3. Fifty-four Forty or Fight
4. King's X Variation
5. Double Star Flower
6. Ohio Star
7. Jacob's Ladder
8. Card Tricks
9. Weathervane
10. Brick Walk
11. Spools
12. Glow Shine
13. Inside Square
14. Ocean Waves
15. Star Flower
16. Gathering Geese
17. Swirl
18. Mexican Star

Borders: 1½″ wide (cut 2″ wide)
Outside border: 2½″ wide (cut 3″ wide)
Fabric requirement: Divide amount needed by color and number of fabrics used.
  Blocks: 2 yards
  Borders: 1½ yards
  Center panel: 2½ yards
  Backing: 5 yards

## STAR BRIGHT

When my son Paul suggested that I finish the blocks featured on the cover of *Lap Quilting*, my first book, I decided to leave them suspended on the deep blue-green field and frame them with a contrasting red paisley. It became a small quilt, perfect for a wall hanging, lap throw, or crib quilt. (The block, Another Star, features a subtle shift between two main colors, that is emphasized with elongated borders.) Triangles and rectangles were sewn together to make the colorful pieced borders. (Figure 7.) The borders were then attached to the quilt using the "stack, sew, and extend" method. (See Added Borders, Chapter 3.) I used both machine and hand quilting throughout the quilt.

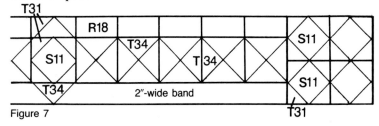

Figure 7

Figure 8. *Star Bright*

***Star Bright*** (photograph on page 21)
Finished quilt: 60″ x 76″ (Figure 8)
Perimeter: 7½′ (272″)
Blocks: Four 12″ blocks (Another Star)
Mitered borders: 3″ x 18″ (cut 3½″ x 19″)
Border around center square: 3¼″ wide (cut
   3¾″ x 43½″)
Corner triangles: 22″ x 22″ x 31″ (cut 4)
Outside border: Across the top and bottom 8″ x
   44″; along the sides 8″ x 76″
Fabric requirements: Divide amount needed by
   color and number of fabrics used.
  Blocks: 1½ yards
  Borders: 2½ yards
  Backing: 4 yards

## TEACHING THE SAMPLER QUILT

The sampler quilt is a perfect teaching tool because it includes such a wide variety of skills. With the addition of each sampler block, new techniques are explored and fabric decisions made. When teaching a class, plan a weekly "show and tell." Encourage students to share their successes *and* failures. Use of slides can also broaden students' horizons.

The following teaching guide may be a useful outline to help keep you on track, whether you are teaching a group or yourself. I have listed the subjects that I would teach week by week. Information about each of the topics can be found throughout *More Lap Quilting*.

***Eight-Week Lesson Plan***

**Week #1:**
  Quilt definitions
  Block setting options
  Fabric: amounts and study of color
  Tools of the trade: notions needed
**Week #2:**
  Drafting exercise with basic four patch
  Template preparation and transfer to fabric
  Three blocks demonstrated (examples:
    King's X, Double Star Flower, Spools)
  Quick piecing with squares and triangles
**Week #3:**
  Drafting exercise with basic nine patch
  Three blocks demonstrated (examples: An-
    other Star, Shoo Fly, Ohio Star)
  Border application
  Where to quilt—stencil application
**Week #4:**
  Batting, backing, and basting
  Lap quilting (with and without a hoop)
  A foolproof knot
  25-patch block description
**Week #5:**
  Curves in patchwork
  Two blocks demonstrated (examples: Drunk-
    ard's Path, Grandmother's Fan)
  Machine-quilting options
**Week #6:**
  Picture blocks
  Basket, houses
  Block-to-block connection
**Week #7:**
  Row connection
  Appliqué demonstration
**Week #8:**
  Border treatments
  Finishing touches—bias binding
  Signature

# The Back Door Block

The most common complaint I hear as a quilting teacher is, "I can't seem to do anything original or different." To answer this need, I have developed a workshop to help the student create her own distinctive block.

When using the traditional, or "front door" approach to block construction, you choose a design and piece a block using a previously drafted pattern. Forget this approach for a moment and follow me through the "back door"—an entryway to creating your own designs.

With the "back door" approach, you do the piecing first and then the designing of the block. Think of a square, and all the possible geometric shapes that could be sewn together to form that square, such as rectangles, triangles, trapezoids, and parallelograms. (Squares are used as the basis of the design because they are so easy to sew together to make your block.) Combine coordinating fabrics and the "quick-piecing" formula; mix and match your squares; and you'll have a truly one-of-a-kind design. You can create an entire quilt such as *Patchfun Shuffle,* or just a border.

## QUICK-PIECING METHODS

The key to the "back door" and to designing your own block is quick-piecing. Five different quick-piecing techniques are included here. If you want to experiment with all of them, you will need one yard each of three coordinating fabrics. You will want them to be contrasting in color. Why cut apart and piece together two small calicoes with the same color tone?

### Rectangles

Stack two contrasting, but compatible, fabrics with right sides together. Cut two strips (one from each fabric), 2″ wide and 45″ long, on the crosswise or lengthwise grain of your fabric. Sew one side of these strips together with a ¼″ seam. Mark and cut apart every 3½″ (or use template R5). (Figure 1.) Press the seam allowance toward the darker fabric. Save these shapes to use later to achieve your desired design or pattern. To expand this idea, as in the blocks of the quilt *Rail Fence* or the rectangular pieced border of *Mexican Star* (both on page 49), sew a band with the desired number of colors and cut apart.

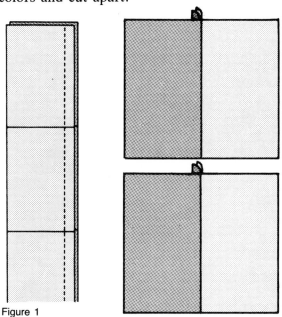

Figure 1

### Four Patch

To form a simple four patch, stack two contrasting, but compatible, fabrics with right sides together. Cut four strips (two from each fabric), 2″ wide and 45″ long, on the crosswise or lengthwise grain of the fabric. Sew two strips of contrasting fabrics together (as you did the rectangles) with ¼″ seams. Repeat for the other two strips. Open each strip and press the seam toward the darker fabric.

Align these two strips, right sides together, with colors reversed and seams staggered. On the back of the fabric, measure and mark off every 2″ with a solid line; you may use the width of a rectangular template as a guide. Now mark a broken line ¼″ to the left (or right—be consistent) of each solid line; stitch along each broken line. Cut on the solid lines to reveal 3½″ four-patch squares. (Figure 2.)

This technique works for a nine patch as well, if you sew one set of bands of dark, light, dark, and then sew together one set of bands of light, dark, light. Then proceed, following instructions for the four patch.

### Triangles into Squares

To form a square from two right-angle triangles, place the right sides of two 8″-square pieces of contrasting fabric together. On the back of one of the fabrics, trace around a triangle T37. Do this in a continuous manner by flipping the template as you trace. Mark a broken line or stitching guide ¼″ from each side of each diagonal line; or use the guide on the presser foot to establish a ¼″ seam allowance as you sew. Cut apart on the solid lines to reveal eight 3½″ squares. (Figure 3.)

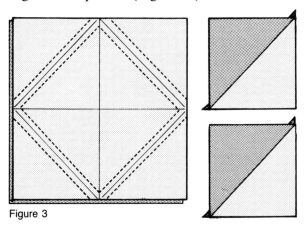

Figure 3

By using a small triangle, such as triangle T5, the exercise above would create 2″ squares. Eight of these tiny triangles can be used to build a 3½″ pinwheel, such as the one in the block Old MacDonald's Farm. When two of these squares are sewn together, they can resemble Flying Geese with an extra seam in the middle.

### Triangles into Triangles

To form a large triangle from two smaller right-angle triangles, place the right sides of two 4½″-wide strips of contrasting fabrics together. On the back of one fabric trace around triangle T24. Do this in a continuous manner by flipping the template as you trace. Place the long side of

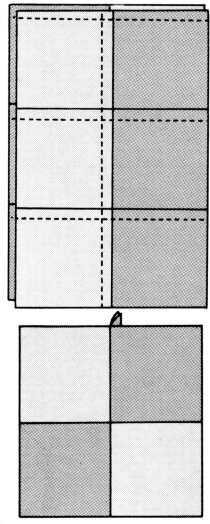

Figure 2

the triangle on the straight of grain or crosswise grain of the fabric. Mark stitching lines ¼″ on both sides of only one diagonal line within each square. (Figure 4.) Sew along the broken lines. Cut apart on *all* solid lines.

To form squares from these pieced triangles, align raw edges, stagger seams, and sew together using ¼″ seam allowances. (Figure 4.)

To make offset squares, the same triangles may be used. Machine-stitch next to *both* diagonal lines and cut apart on the solid lines.

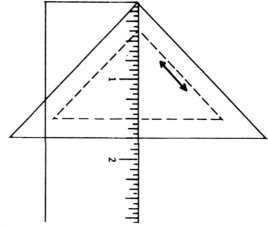

Figure 5

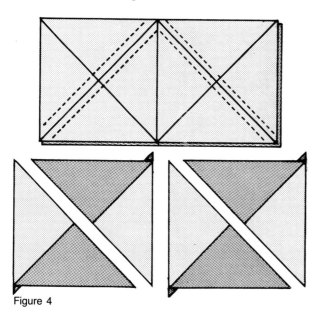

Figure 4

### Flying Geese

The Flying Geese rectangle is composed of two sizes of triangles cut from contrasting fabrics. By taking advantage of the fact that the smaller triangle is sewn on the bias, this popular design can be made using a quick-piecing method.

Cut out the large triangles, using triangle T24. (Remember, they must contrast with the smaller triangles.) Instead of cutting out your small triangles, cut a bias strip. To figure the width of your bias strip, measure the height of the small triangle from the right angle to the point directly opposite. The height of triangle T5 is 1¾″. (Figure 5.)

The length of your bias strip will depend on the size of the large triangle you are using. Every triangle T24 requires a 5″ length of bias, so if you are making 12 Flying Geese rectangles, you will need a bias strip 60″ or 1⅔ yards long.

Using the above calculations, you can now cut a bias strip 1¾″ wide by 60″ long. With right sides together, pin the bias edge of each triangle T24 along this bias strip, leaving ½″ between the triangles. Sew with a ¼″ seam. (Figure 6.) Cut through the bias strip along the hypotenuse of each triangle. You now have a parallelogram sewn to one side of triangle T24.

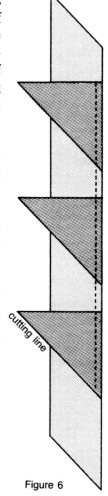

cutting line

Figure 6

Unfold the pieces and place right side up. Use the small triangle T5 as a guide to cut the parallelogram in half and form a second, companion triangle. (Figure 7.) Sew the hypotenuse of the second triangle to the other side of triangle T24 to complete the unit. (Figure 8.) Rectangle R5 can be used as the master template to check the accuracy of your Flying Geese unit.

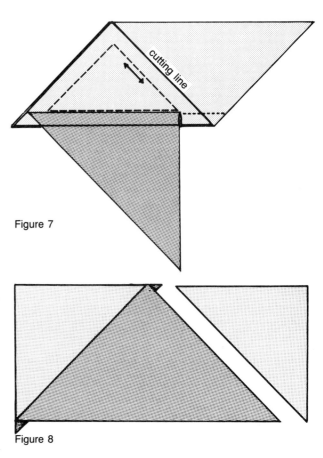

Figure 7

Figure 8

Now that you've tried the basic quick-piecing exercise, play with the placement of the shapes you have made. Shifting and turning these new shapes will reveal many new designs. It may be necessary to add squares or rectangles for emphasis or balance. Keep graph paper nearby for sketching and planning. Arrange your shapes on a flannel board or felt board and let them "age" just in case you want to change your design.

The most successful workshop I have taught on quick-piecing methods was the result of a delay brought on by a snowstorm. The students had time to juggle the pieced shapes for some time, and many invited their families to help with the geometric arrangements. Perhaps there are two important lessons here: Don't rush into your decisions, and do let your family be involved!

### *PATCHFUN SHUFFLE*

Once, several years ago, a quilt top I truly admired slipped through my fingers. I always referred to it as "the one that got away"; however, I was fortunate enough to get a picture of it. It was a sampler of sorts with jumbled geometric shapes, perhaps the piecework from a lifetime of leftovers. That quilt top provided the impetus for an arrangement of shapes in the quilt I call *Patchfun Shuffle*.

A close examination of my *Patchfun Shuffle* quilt reveals the unexpected—words, in this case sentences, machine-stitched on the top! (I simply had something to say, and with machine quilting I realized I could quilt a message on

each light-colored panel.) The words are marked with a water-erasable pen, which makes removal easy after the machine work is completed. The matching bobbin thread blends into the rust background. The panels of geometric shapes saved from many quick-piecing workshops are machine-quilted in a "wandering scribble." (I just meandered—feed dogs down—starting in the center of each panel, creating gentle loops, angles, and other designs that came to mind.)

The finishing touch is the pleated ruffle that makes a soft, gentle accent.

*Patchfun Shuffle* (photograph on page 3)
Finished quilt: 81″ x 96″ without ruffle, 85″ x 100″ with ruffle
Perimeter: 10 yards (354″)
Panels: 9″ x 96″ (cut 9½″ x 96″), four panels with geometric shapes, five with writing
Ruffle: 2″ double ruffle
Fabric requirements:
  Panels: 3 yards of solid fabric, 3 yards of pieced fabric
  Backing: 6 yards
  Ruffle: 15 yards, cut 4½″ wide

# The Flexicurve Formula

Who would have guessed that a drafting tool used by architects would introduce me to a whole new world of quilting designs! I bought my first flexible curve or "flexicurve" as I call it at a college bookstore. I found that it enabled me to quickly "sew and flip" many undulating curves in succession. This tool can also be useful when you are stenciling curved quilting lines or drafting curves in pattern design. The flexicurve is made of plastic with an interior metal core. It is ½″ wide at the wider portion, the base, and comes in various lengths. (Quarter-inch seam allowances on matching sides of the curve equal the ½″ base measurement of the flexicurve.)

Using the flexicurve, I have developed a wonderful form of crazy patch that is actually the simple sew-and-flip method done on a foundation cut from Pellon fleece, muslin, or any scrap material. Remember that the foundation fabric must be preshrunk and pressed, along with the other fabrics you are using. Although the foundation is never seen, it should not be darker than the design fabrics that are sewn on top, because it could show through and alter the other colors. Be sure to cut the foundation ½″ larger than the desired finished size, as some take-up does occur as you sew and flip.

All of the star centers in *Stars Over the Smokies* were constructed using the flexicurve formula. Cut a muslin foundation from the large circle template Sp17. Four to twelve colors were used in each of my "fabric-scapes."

### SEW-AND-FLIP FLEXICURVE

Place the piece of fabric you have chosen for the top of your design on the foundation, right side up. Pin it in place. Bend the flexicurve into the desired shape. Keep in mind that the deeper or sharper the curve, the more difficult it will be to sew. Place the flexicurve on the fabric. Mark with chalk the top of the flexicurve tool to indicate where you want this portion of the design to start and stop. Now trace the curves onto the fabric along the *bottom edge* of the

flexicurve, starting and stopping at the chalk lines marked on the flexicurve. (Figure 1.) Use a pencil, water-erasable pen, or a soap sliver, depending on the color of your fabric. (If you are making a garment and want identical patterns on each side, work in duplicate with the wrong sides of the fabrics together.) Mark the chalk lines on your fabric above the flexicurve.

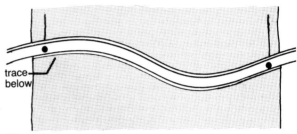

Figure 1

Lift off the flexicurve, being careful not to alter its shape. Cut the fabric along this traced curved line, but do not cut the foundation material. Discard the bottom scrap of fabric.

Without altering the shape of the flexicurve, place it toward the top part of your second fabric. This does not have to be on the straight of grain. This time, trace along the *top edge* of the flexicurve, starting and stopping at the chalk lines marked on the flexicurve. Mark the chalk lines on your fabric above the flexicurve. These marks are start-and-stop guidelines. (Figure 2.)

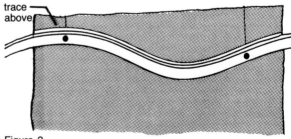

Figure 2

From the top of the second piece of fabric, cut down the chalk lines; then cut along the traced line and discard the top of the fabric. The first and second fabrics will fit together like a puzzle.

Cut down an additional ¼″ at the start-and-stop guidelines to release the seam allowance. Pin the right sides of both fabrics together, matching the raw edges of the curves, and the chalk marks. (Figure 3.)

Machine-sew through all three layers (both fabric pieces and foundation) with a ¼″ seam allowance. (Stitch slowly around sharp curves and make sure the needle is down as you turn to help stabilize the fabric.) After sewing, clip the seam at any taut area and press it lightly to one side. Trim along the edges of the foundation. (Figure 4.)

Continue to add new fabrics in this manner, altering the shapes of the curves by bending or shaping the flexicurve after each fabric addition. Consider inserting appliquéd figures into the curves, such as a sun, a flower, or a house. To achieve a variety of effects, try different fabrics. Sheer fabrics create a gentle illusion while heavy fabrics can provide interesting textures. The flexicurve formula can be used to create many interesting designs to enhance belts, a jacket, and even an attaché case. (See the photographs on pages 80 and 51.)

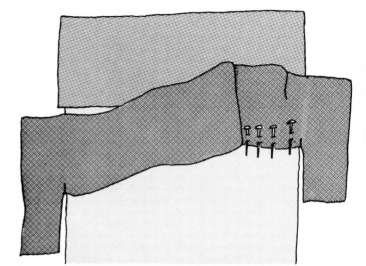

Figure 3

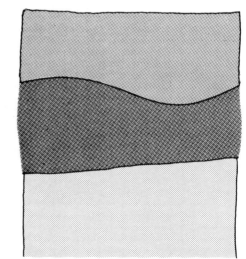

Figure 4

**Opposite:** *Green squares and quilted clovers angle across* Double Irish Chain *as it airs in the summer sun.*

*Every child has a favorite quilt. In* Stacking Spools Baby Quilt, *even the quilting is done on the machine.*

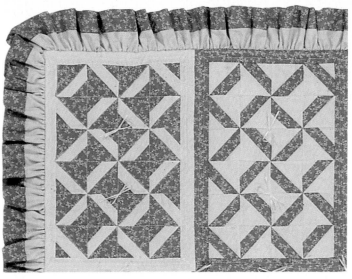

**Opposite:** *The block-to-block arrangement in* Grandmother's Fan *creates a new design. The same colors flow into a rectangular border.*

*A center nine patch radiates outward in* Mexican Star *to form an unusual elongated star while a colorful border frames the quilt.*

*The colors of autumn leaves seem to zigzag across* Rail Fence *to the light band that separates the quilt from the border.*

**Opposite:** *Many brown scraps make these variations on a theme in* Brown Stars. *The quilt has a double life because each star block has a different calico backing—a reversible quilt!*

With the flexicurve and my sewing machine, I enhanced my favorite jacket pattern with curved piecing at the yoke and cuffs.

A rainbow of colors and the flexi-curve create an attractive attaché case.

Virginia's Choice *is a traditional quilt pattern that is sometimes called Hearts and Gizzards.*

**Opposite:** *In* Tulips and Bluebells, *contrasting flowers and leaves of two shades of green give a fresh look to an appliqué pattern.*

## STARS OVER THE SMOKIES

The overall design for my *Stars Over the Smokies* quilt is based on a block with a single border and square corner inserts. However, two rectangles (the size of two combined squares) make an interesting break in the repetition of the squares. I highlighted the rectangular panels with houses and other appliquéd features.

### Piecing the Star Block

On the back of your "fabric-scape" picture draw a perfect circle, using template Sp17. Mark the eight divisions shown on the template on the back of your circle to help you later when you are aligning the star-point unit.

Set the circle aside and sew the sides of the star points (Sp10) to the sides of the four triangles (T25). Next, sew the corner squares (S2) to the star points. This will complete the star-point unit surrounding your circle. (Figure 5.)

Lay the pieced star unit face down. Lay the fabric-scape on top, face down, matching the

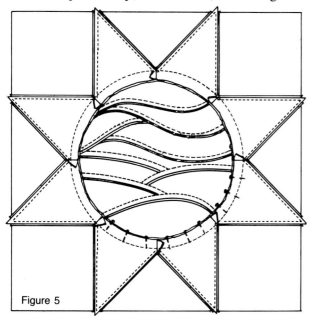

Figure 5

**Opposite:** Stars Over the Smokies *presents a variety of landscapes created with the flexicurve and the sew-and-flip method.*

eight intersections you marked on the circle to the eight seams on the star points. Pinch the ¼" seam allowances, right sides together, and pin. Sew all the way around the circle easing any excess. (Figure 5.)

Instead of lap-quilting each square, sew the blocks together to make rectangles and then lap-quilt each of the ten sections. (Figure 6.) Notice that borders are not on all blocks.

*Stars Over the Smokies* (photograph on page 52)
Finished quilt: 74" x 92"
Perimeter: 9½ yards (332")
Blocks: Sixteen 16" squares
    Muslin foundation: Sixteen circles (Template Sp17—cut with extra fullness)
    Star points: Cut 128
    Squares: Cut 64
    Triangles: Cut 64
Rectangular blocks: Two, 34½" x 16½" (cut muslin foundations 36" x 17")
Borders: 2" x 16" (cut 47 strips, 2½" x 16½")
Border inserts: 2" squares (cut 30, 2½" squares)
Fabric requirements: Divide amount needed by number and colors of fabrics used.
    Stars: 2 yards
    Borders: 1½ yards
    Backing: 5 yards

## THE FLEXICURVE ATTACHÉ CASE
(photograph on page 51)

**Materials**

2 (19″ x 13″) rectangular pieces of foundation
    fabric
2 (18½″ x 12½″) rectangular pieced blocks
2 (10″ x 2½″) pieces of batting for handles
2 (18½″ x 12½″) pieces of batting
2 (18½″ x 12½″) pieces of backing material (use
    a dark color because it will show less soil)
1 (18″) heavy-duty zipper
1 (1⅔ yards long x 2½″ wide) length of bias
    strip for binding and handles

**Method**

Cut the foundation for your attaché case
slightly larger than the desired finished size to
allow for the take-up that will occur as you sew
and flip. Select an array of different-colored
fabrics. Cut them out using your flexicurve to
determine the degree of your curves. Once the
rectangles are pieced, baste your rectangle, batting, and lining together. A firm batting will
help make this a sturdy case. Quilt each rectangle by hand or by machine.

To make the handles, cut two 10″ lengths of
bias strip. Place a length of selvage or a shoelace on the right side of each piece of bias,
making sure it extends from each end of the bias
strip. Fold the bias strip in half with right sides
together and raw edges aligned. (Shoelace or
selvage is inside.)

Place a piece of batting under the folded
bias strip against the feed dogs of the machine.
Machine-stitch the bias strip and batting together across one end (so that the selvage or
shoelace is caught) and along the side. Pull the
selvage piece from the open end of the folded
bias tube and invert the entire handle. The
handle may be left as is, or you can add several
rows of machine-stitching lines for accent. Attach the handle in place 5″ from each end, with

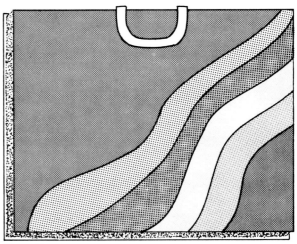

Figure 7

the raw edges of the handles aligned with the
raw edges of the rectangles. (Figure 7.) Repeat
for other side of case.

Using a zipper-foot attachment, sew the
open zipper to the top edge of one rectangle.
(This will include the handle.) Turn the zipper
back over the raw edge and slip-stitch it in
place. Close the zipper and sew it to the opposite side of the case, right sides together.

As a final step, align the rectangles with
backings together and apply double bias binding around the outside edges. (If you prefer that
the binding not show, align the rectangles with
the right sides together.) Be sure to square off
corners as instructed for quilt corners (Chapter
3). Place a ring in the end of the zipper for ease
in opening.

# Applauding Appliqué

Appliqué: from the French. Definition: to apply (as a decoration or ornament) to a larger surface.

Potential appliqué designs are all around us—in nature, children's coloring books, simple folded-paper cutouts, and of course, in quilts from the past. A study of quilting would not be complete without a study of appliqué. Since there are many ways to appliqué and since we all hold a needle and handle fabric differently, we must test and discover our own favorite method. The severity of the curve or point will often determine the method we use.

### APPLIQUÉ WITHOUT SEAM ALLOWANCE

The simplest form of appliqué is the figure cut without any seam allowance. The edges may be secured by hand or by machine. This method was most often seen in early 20th-century Dutch Girl quilts in which black embroidery thread was used to form very close buttonhole stitches around the figures. (Figure 1.) A certain amount of fraying would start once the figures were handled and used, but eventually it would cease and form a decorative, uniform edge.

### Machine Appliqué

The satin stitch done on a sewing machine can form a very neat, tight edging. (Figure 2.)

The thread color can vary here—a contrast to accent or a match to blend with the appliqué figure. Before sewing, however, secure the cutout figure in position with a spray adhesive or stick glue. This prevents the cutout from shifting while you are sewing. If you are appliquéing a figure to a single thickness of fabric, it helps to have a stabilizer underneath, because machine satin stitches tend to draw the material.

The open embroidery presser foot or an all-purpose presser foot can be aligned with the raw edge to provide a stitching guide. To achieve the proper width and length of your zigzag stitch, always do a test sample first. With this type of presser foot, it is important to note the position of the needle at right-angle turns. For outside right-angle turns, pivot with the needle on the outside or right side. For inside right-angle turns, pivot with the needle on the inside or left side.

You will need to alter the width of the satin stitch as you sew, to make adjustments for acute corners such as those found in star or leaf points. Narrow the satin stitch as you approach any sharp angles. Turn and slowly widen the stitches as you move away from the point area. When finished, pull the loose top thread to the back and tie off. To give elevation and emphasis to the satin stitch, lay a narrow piece of cord along the edge and satin-stitch over it.

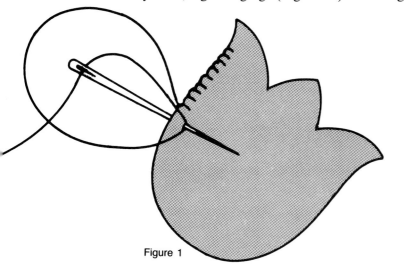

Figure 1

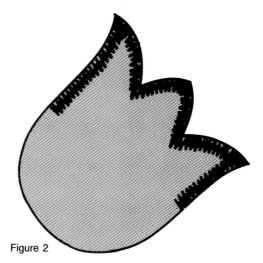

Figure 2

*Appliqué and seminole patchwork enhance this jacket pattern.*

### APPLIQUÉ WITH SEAM ALLOWANCE

Most forms of appliqué have a seam allowance or ¼″ extension that needs to be turned under to form a smooth, finished edge. A template that includes seam allowances is used to cut out the appliqué figure. If the template is made from plastic, you can see through it to position it according to the design of the fabric.

Another template, without seam allowances, can also be a good tool. Trace around it on the foundation fabric to make a guide for turning under the raw edges of the appliqué figure. This also shows you where to position the appliqué. Another way to make a guide for turning under raw edges is to trace around the template on the actual appliqué figure that was cut with seam allowances.

If you place this second template on top of the appliqué figure and iron the seam allowances back over the template, you form a crease. This shows you how far to turn under the raw edge. Spray starch helps set this pressed curve. (If you use this technique, make sure the template is made of cardboard or freezer paper—not plastic.)

Appliqué seams are treated in a variety of ways. The ¼″ seam allowance can be basted under with a contrasting thread. Work with the back of the figure facing you and the knot on the front for easy removal. On curved seams, clip any concave seams and notch the fullness out of convex seams. A simple machine stay stitch sewn right next to the finished edge adds weight to the appliqué figure and makes the turn-under easier and more exact.

You may wish to add a stem stitch worked by hand along the finished edge (¼″ from the raw edge). This will form a neat edge after the seam allowance is turned under.

Double appliqué is actually a double thickness of fabric—the appliqué figure and a facing.

Align the right sides of the appliqué figure and the facing and sew all the way around them with a ¼″ seam allowance. Trim and clip all seams for a smooth finish. Snip a small opening in the facing and turn the figure right side out; press flat before applying the figure to the foundation fabric. (Figure 3.)

## SEWING THE APPLIQUÉ

The slip stitch is the usual stitch for attaching appliqué figures to a foundation or base fabric. (A whipstitch doesn't work because loose threads will catch and wear out.) A proper slip stitch is worked from right to left. The needle is pulled up through the block or foundation fabric and catches only a few threads of the folded edge of the appliqué figure. Each time the needle is inserted in the block, it should be under the top thread of the edge of the appliqué figure. (Figure 4.) This keeps the thread from angling. You should have long single strands of thread showing on the back, but very little, if any, thread should be visible on the front.

Once the figures are slip-stitched in place, you can add an accent line of stem stitching at the very edge.

The appliqué figure can also be attached by basting the figure in position and then, with the point of the needle, turning the seam under as you slip-stitch the figure in place. This method takes practice and careful basting. It helps to draw the figure first on the foundation or block as a guide.

Using a close, tiny running stitch at the very edge of the turned-under seam allowance is another simple, yet effective, way to appliqué. Use thread that blends with the fabric.

If your sewing machine has a blind hem stitch, you might use it to appliqué. Set the presser foot very close to the folded edge. Sew a series of small stitches on the foundation fabric or block, and then catch the turned-under edge of the appliqué figure with one short zigzag stitch. Use a clear polyfilament thread to disguise any stitches.

The above techniques can also be used with reverse appliqué, Hawaiian appliqué, and shadow trapunto. These are in the category of novelty work and can be very effective used alone or mixed with other techniques.

The most popular quilting lines for appliqué echo the shape of the figure, although cross-hatching and other straight lines do help to accent the shapes sometimes. The two appliqué quilts, *Tri-State Tulip, Tulips and Bluebells*, and the wall hanging, *Romance of the Roses*, were done by turning under the seam allowance and slip-stitching the edge in place.

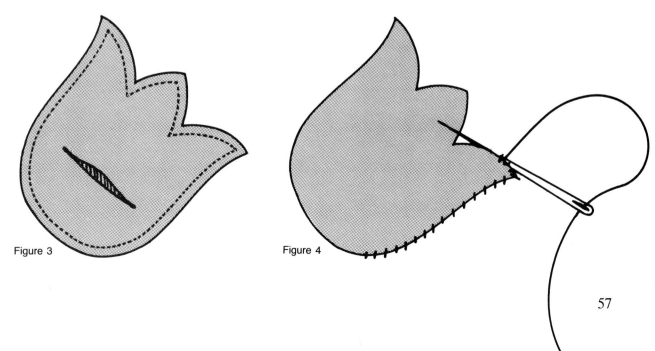

Figure 3

Figure 4

## TRI-STATE TULIP

Three generations of women from three states have stitched and enhanced this quilt, with its alluring appliqué. When the quilt *Tri-State Tulip* came to me, the pieces were in progress. Through lap quilting we were able to complete the quilt.

Two sets of borders frame each of the 8″-square appliqué blocks. A 1″ border along with a 2″ border forms the 3″-wide border that surrounds the block on four sides. The three sections of the outside 14″-wide border are quilted separately and added after the center of the quilt is assembled. (Figure 5.)

*Tri-State Tulip* (photograph on page 26)
Finished quilt: 70″ x 84″
Perimeter: 9 yards (308″)
Appliqué blocks: Seventeen 14″ blocks
Appliqué block borders: Inside border 1″, outside border 2″
Side borders for quilt: 14″ (cut 2½″, 10½″, 2½″ x 70½″)
End borders for quilt: 14″ (cut 2½″, 10½″, 2½″ x 42½″ plus two 14″ blocks at each end)
Fabric requirements: Divide the amount needed by the number and colors of fabric used.
   Blocks: 1½ yards
   Borders: 2½ yards of each of the two colors
   Backing: 5 yards

## TULIPS AND BLUEBELLS

It's a surprise to see the strong impact just two simple appliqué figures can have on a white surface. Embroidery has been combined with the appliqué in the quilt *Tulip and Bluebells* to create a fresh-flowing design.

After you have appliquéd each of your 10″-square blocks, sew them together in groups of four to form twenty 20″ squares. With a stem stitch, embroider the stems using all six strands

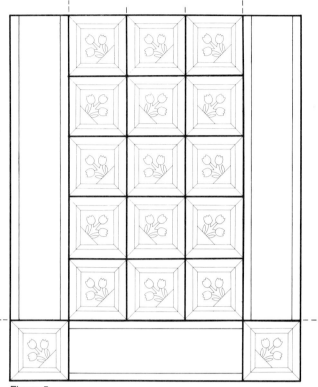

Figure 5

of embroidery thread. Do not stitch all the way to the edge of the block however. Leave the threads dangling until all the blocks are joined. Then you can continue embroidering.

Cut the foundation and batting the same size as the 20″-square block. Baste all three layers together and quilt as one unit. By doing this you will have fewer seams in your backing.

*Tulips and Bluebells* (photograph on page 50)
Finished quilt: 80″ x 100″
Perimeter: 10 yards (360″)
Appliqué blocks: Twenty 20″ squares (four 10″ squares for each block)
Fabric requirements: Divide the amount needed by the number and colors of fabrics used.
Appliqué blocks: 2 yards for flowers, ½ yard for leaves
Foundation: 6 yards
Backing: 6 yards

## ROMANCE OF THE ROSES

Traditional Christmas colors of red and green give this wall hanging a seasonal look. But it is certainly too beautiful to display only once a year.

It will be easier to appliqué the many small pieces in each of the blocks in *Romance of the Roses* if you do some preliminary marking. Fold the 12″-square foundation material and crease it so that you have eight divisions marked. (Figure 6.) These divisions act as a guide when positioning the appliqué pieces. If you are working with a circular design, draw a circle on your foundation fabric in addition to creasing. For example in the block Presidents's Wreath, draw an 8½″ circle; in North Carolina Rose, draw a 7½″ circle to provide a guide for positioning the ½″ bias strips.

Figure 7

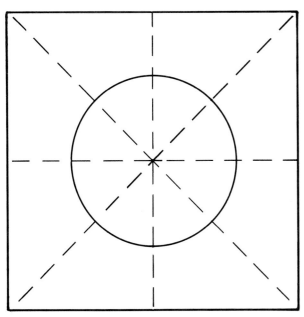

Figure 6

To make the borders that surround each block, sew together a band of three strips, cut 1½″ wide and 8½ yards long. Then cut this strip into 24 borders 12½″ long. Add the corner inserts between your border pieces before you sew the borders to the blocks. Use templates

A7 and A22 to cut out the small appliquéd flowers in the four inserts surrounding the center block. Nine-patch inserts are used in the other corners. The blocks in the top and bottom rows of the quilt have four borders attached. The blocks in the middle row share these borders, so only side borders are sewn to the middle row of blocks. (Figure 7.)

***Romance of the Roses*** (photograph on page 25)
Finished quilt: 48″ x 48″
Perimeter: 5½ yards (192″)
Appliqué blocks: Nine 12″ blocks
Borders: 3″ wide (3 strips cut 1½″ wide x 8½ yards long)
Border inserts: Twelve 3″ nine-patch inserts and four 3″ appliquéd inserts
Fabric requirements:
  Black: 1 yard
  Green: 1¼ yards
  Red: 1 yard
  Tan: ¼ yard
  Foundation: 1¼ yards
  Backing: 2¾ yards

# Guilds and Groups

It's enjoyable to quilt every week at a church get-together or in a friend's home, but the benefits of an organized guild are enormous. The give-and-take between members, the opportunity to import professionals, the impact on your community through charitable endeavors and business growth are all bonuses.

## GET ORGANIZED

- Post a sign-up sheet in the library, community center, and in retail stores. A quilt design used in the graphics of your poster will catch the eye of quilters.
- Start with a nucleus of serious, experienced quilters to set the initial guidelines.
- Find a meeting place such as a church or library room. Decide on the time and dates to meet. Check other ongoing activities to avoid scheduling conflicts.
- Advertise your meeting time and place in the local papers and on radio and TV well in advance of the first meeting.

*The Landrum Library Quilters*

**At the first meeting try to accomplish the following things:**
- Establish goals.
- Decide on an official name.
- Elect officers—President, Vice President (usually in charge of the programs, guest speakers and workshops), Secretary, Treasurer, Parliamentarian, and chairpersons.
- Decide on a membership fee.
- Choose day and time for meetings—consider alternating day and evening meetings every month in order to catch both the working person and the person who doesn't care to drive in the evening.
- Make a membership list by recording names and addresses in a guest book.

**Newly formed guilds should:**
- Establish a bank account.
- Contact local IRS to discuss nonprofit status.
- Write bylaws—the operating rules.
- Determine how to raise funds to build a treasury. This could include a quilt show, lectures, or a raffle of a group quilt.
- Solicit a local adult-education department at a technical school or college, an arts council, or a local government agency in the community for support and endorsement.

## DO'S AND DON'TS FOR GUILD PROJECTS

"Many hands make light work" is truly an applicable saying when a quilt becomes a group effort. The group, united for a common goal, divides the amount of labor and multiplies the pride and satisfaction of accomplishment. But the problems created by dealing with a variety of skilled craftsmen must be anticipated.

**Do** start with plenty of time to spare. Allow at least 10 to 12 months for total production of your guild quilt.

**Do** evaluate the expertise of the group. Are they beginners, intermediates, or advanced quilters?

**Do** work out the entire design on paper first. This becomes a drafting lesson for all to learn. Check all templates to be sure they are sturdy and accurate.

**Do** assign deadlines and goals so that people know when projects are due.

**Do** make certain all fabric is prewashed and buy extra to allow for mishaps.

**Do** keep an up-to-date list of names, addresses, and phone numbers of all involved.

**Do** keep time charts to evaluate the amount of time spent on the project.

**Don't** bite off more than you can sew, or you will find members falling by the wayside.

**Don't** hurt anyone's feelings. It is better to rip out and redo in private than to embarrass a fellow quilter.

**Don't** wait until too late to assemble the blocks in preparation for the finishing touches.

As chairman of the group quilt for the Western North Carolina Quilters Guild's annual show, my final responsibility was to submit a report to the show chairman. This report outlined our schedule and the procedure we followed to complete our quilt. Maybe it will help you plan your next guild project.

*About ten months before the quilt show, I did a survey and study of the North Carolina Lily patterns. It showed that most of the patterns were based on an eight-pointed star and were red, white, and green. This helped me choose our pattern. Another thing that helped our pattern choice was that all of our group—150 members—had quilted before and were at an intermediate level. I drafted the pattern and showed it to the group. No "boos," so we used that pattern and worked on dividing the piecing so that all could be involved.*

*At a meeting eight months before the deadline, I gave out sets of four muslin diamonds to many eager hands. The lily quilt required 41 sets of four diamonds! Since the lily diamonds were to be string-pieced, the muslin was cut larger than the template to allow for take-up. During a*

*demonstration of string piecing, I pleaded with everyone to preshrink all red fabrics and to eliminate any fabric that continued to fade or bleed. We gave one set of four diamonds to each quilter so that the same quilter would do one entire flower. Deadlines were assigned so that each quilter would know when her lily was to be completed. Several group meetings were used to trim the completed diamonds, pencil the corner turns on the back, complete the 20½" square, and "ooh" and "aah" over the results.*

*The 20½" squares of muslin that were set between the lily blocks were not pieced; they were only quilted. Many hours and cups of coffee were required to mark the elaborate stencil design on these squares. A muted calico backing was chosen and cut, using a large cardboard template. Because the lily blocks and the stencil design blocks were set on point, the backing had to be cut with the straight of the grain on the diagonal. That left all four sides of the backing cut on the bias.*

*The stems for the pieced blocks were made with ½" bias bars and passed on to the best appliqué artists in our guild.*

*Before long "flying fingers" were at work. Each quilter was cautioned to trim any excess thread or any dark green or red fabric that overlapped the white seam allowances.*

*Just imagine 24 different quilters doing their own stitching on 24 sections that would later be assembled as one quilt! To avoid a problem, guide sheets were given to each quilter, indicating exactly where to place the quilting lines so that all blocks would look reasonably alike. They were reminded to leave at least ½" free of quilting around the outside of each block. This allowed for the block-to-block assembly later on.*

*Pleas for help from the chairman brought people to the rescue when the deadline was near. After blocks were trimmed, rows were assembled by a committee of one. (Parts of any guild effort do lend themselves better to a committee of one!) The quilt was bound in white. A soft frame held the names of all who had helped.*

## STRING ALONG LILY

"Strings" used to be the long extras left over from making a quilt or a garment. They could be regular or irregular in shape. If these pieces happened to be large or odd shapes, they were cut into separate long pieces, regardless of grain or bias. Strings were precious and were held aside for a special purpose—to be string-pieced either on a paper or a cloth foundation. The foundation was cut the size of the template including seam allowances.

Today, this same method is used, but we are occasionally guilty of taking a perfectly good, whole piece of cloth and cutting it up to look like strings. Some might consider this foolish, but if you are a quilter, you know this is an accepted fiber art process—legitimate and legal.

This quilt was named for the string-pieced lily diamonds. *String Along Lily* is a testament to the dedication of the quilters, and shows what can be accomplished with good organization and a concentrated group effort.

The strings are applied using the sew-and-flip technique. Start with a string that will cover the length of the foundation—either straight across (as was done with our lily diamonds), lengthwise, or on the diagonal.

Pin the first string in place right side up, in the center of the foundation. Place the second piece on top of the first, right sides together and raw edges aligned on one side. With a ¼″ seam allowance, sew through both strings and the foundation. Flip the second piece back to reveal the right side and thumb-crease or press it in place. (Figure 1.) Position pins every 3 to 3½″ to prevent any pulling as the next string is attached. Continue this sew-and-flip procedure until the foundation is covered. You may trim as you go, or wait until the last string has been added to cut off any excess material around the foundation.

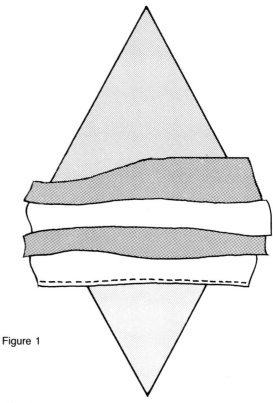

Figure 1

### Piecing the Lily Blocks

Trim all the string-pieced diamonds and mark ¼″ inside each angle on the back of the diamonds. Arrange all the pieces for one block with the triangles and squares around the diamonds. Sew all the lilies, stopping at the corner turns and backstitching. Set in the small white triangles and the corner squares, backstitching once again at all inside right angles. (Figure 2.) Attach the green base to each lily, extending the dog ears equally on each side.

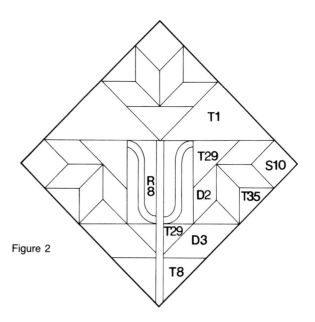

Figure 2

Sew the large white triangles on both sides of the central lily. This completes the top section of the block.

To complete the center section of the block, sew the two remaining lilies to each side of the center rectangle. Do not stitch the place where the stems will be inserted at the top corners of the rectangle.

To assemble the bottom section of the block, attach the leaves to the small white center triangle. Then sew this completed section to the base triangle.

Sew the bottom section to the center section of the block. Use the flexicurve to mark the curved position for the ½″ bias stem. Appliqué the curved stem in place, along with the straight center stem. Attach the top section with the single lily to complete the block. Assemble a total of nine lily blocks.

**Piecing the Border**

Assemble the pieced band, using four string-pieced diamonds and three white triangles. Sew the large white trapezoid to the long side of the pieced band. Sew the large white triangle to the other side of the band. (Figure 3.) Make a total of 14 border sections in this manner. The corner border triangles can be quilted at one time if they have been sewn together to make one large triangle.

Figure 4. *String Along Lily*

***String Along Lily*** (photograph on page 23)
Finished quilt: 84″ x 112″
Perimeter: 11 yards (392″)
Pieced blocks: Nine 20½″ square blocks
Quilted blocks: Eight 20½″ square blocks
Triangular borders: Fourteen
Fabric needed: Divide amount of fabric by colors and number of fabrics used
   Diamonds: 1.5 yards (remnants for string piecing)
   Green leaves and stems: 9½ yards
   Backing: 7 yards
   White for blocks: 6 yards

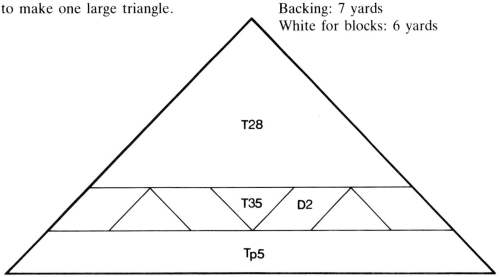

Figure 3

T28

T35  D2

Tp5

## MAIL-A-QUILT

I asked our state quilt board to create a quilt that could be given to our state educational television system. This was to be a gift to express our appreciation for their commitment to the arts.

This time the project was completed with the help of the United States mail. This was a natural group project, because each of the 20 blocks could be completed by a different person. A letter to the quilters introduced the pattern and templates and gave the completion date. And all of this took place without the quilters meeting together!

The quilt is based on 16″-square blocks. Within each 16″-square block is a colorful 12½″-square patchwork center. To make the patchwork go quickly, cut a center strip of gray fabric 2½″ wide and 1½ yards long. With right sides together, sew different-colored blocks to one side of the gray strip, leaving just enough room to cut between blocks. (Figure 5.) We used two yellow blocks, four green, six red, four lavender and two blue for each 12½″ square. If you are going to make the entire quilt yourself, you might want to use the quick-piecing method for four patch. There are nine four-patch blocks in every 12½″ patchwork center.

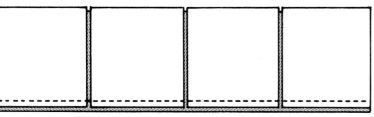

Figure 5

The 12½″ blocks are enlarged to 16″ with the addition of two parallelograms and two triangles. Sew a triangle to one end of each large parallelogram. Insert a folded, gray bias strip (cut 1″ x 6″) between the two parallelograms. Catch the raw edges in the diagonal seam as you sew. The other edge will remain

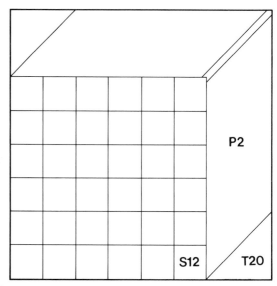

Figure 6

loose. (Figure 6.) Carefully sew your right-angle turn as you attach this unit to the patchwork center.

Two adjoining sides of the outside border are cut from the gray fabric and primary-colored fabrics using P1. The patterns for the other two adjoining sides are T20 and P2. These two sides are cut from all gray and black fabric. We used masking tape for diagonal quilting guidelines. Notice how these lines avoid the bulkiness of seam intersections. A small hoop was used to secure the three layers as we quilted.

The actual design for our quilt was the result of some doodling I had done while talking on the phone. I added knobs and an antenna to a square, and suddenly I had a TV. As the design developed, however, the look of a TV disappeared, and I became concerned that the original concept was lost. But one day, while traveling in Kentucky, I displayed the quilt top to a class and asked for suggestions for a name. A student exclaimed that it looked like a test pattern—and the name seemed to fit!

**_Test Patterns_** (photograph on page 84)
Finished quilt: 88″ x 72″
Perimeter: 9 yards (320″)
Blocks: Twenty 16″ squares
Fabric needed: Divide amount needed by number and colors of fabrics used.
Blocks: 4 yards
Borders: 1½ yards
Backing: 5 yards

## HERE'S THE CHURCH
## AND HERE'S THE STEEPLE

As a child, sitting next to my grandmother in a church pew on Sunday morning, there were some anxious moments—due in large part, I'm sure, to my youthful impatience. But Grandma kept me busy folding the church bulletin into hats and boats, digging into her purse for goodies, and—when all else failed—showing me how to knit fingers to make a tiny church full of "finger people." She would whisper, "Here's the church and here's the steeple; open the door and here's the people."

When my Landrum, South Carolina, quilt club (notice the possessive "my") agreed to help me with a quilt, I told them I wanted to do a picture of a church based on rectangles. The name was a natural, *Here's the Church and Here's the Steeple*, garnered from those wonderful memories of my grandmother and Sunday mornings.

The quilt pattern was first graphed onto paper, divided into rows and then sections. This made it easier to distribute the piecing duties among the club members. Section 1 includes the sky and steeple; section 2 includes the sky, roof line and part of the tree; section 3 includes the windows; section 4, the church and door; section 5 includes the steps leading up to the church. Section 6 completes the wall hanging with the pieced cross border.

The rectangles throughout the quilt are staggered, creating the look of a brick church and an interesting pattern in the sky and foreground. The church is developed in rows. This enables you to alternate the closed seams on every row.

A technique that I refer to as "overlapping piecework" is used to add the steeple. This technique eliminates the need for extra templates. Piece the top three rows, leaving the center seam open. Sew the rows together to form Section 1.

Punch six holes in the steeple template (T12) as indicated on the pattern. Align the center side of the template with the raw edge of one side of Section 1. With a fabric marker, mark points 1, 2, 3, 4, and 5 on the right side of the fabric. (Figure 7.) Flip the template over and do the same on the front of the other half of Section 1. Using the same template, cut out the steeple and mark these same points on the wrong side of the steeple fabric. With right sides together, match the points on the steeple pieces with the points marked on the two pieces of Section 1 and sew together. (Figure 8.) Cut away the extra or the partial rectangles that fall under the steeple. To join Section 1, sew the center seam of the steeple up to point 6. The steeple will extend to the border for emphasis.

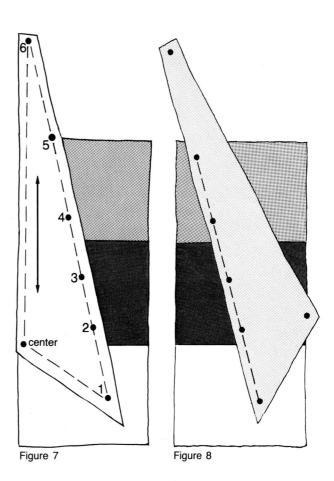

Figure 7          Figure 8

One member of the club volunteered to do the special piecing required for the stained-glass windows. The windows were made as a unit. This unit included the rectangle below each curved section.

For the windows, gather together solid fabrics in radiant stained-glass colors. Cut the fabrics in narrow strips and sew the strips together. Cut this large strip apart and repiece it. Cut R3 and curved piece Sp21 out of this fabric. Sew these shapes together to form the windows. Hand-sew narrow black soutache braid, like the lead in a stain-glassed design, over each seam to accent the various colors. (Figure 9.)

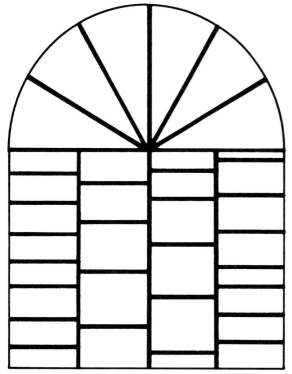

Figure 9

The front double-door section is also made as a unit with a separate 5½″ x 9½″ rectangle cut for the interior. Since the doors swing open, they are lined, quilted, and "hinged." Cut two outside door pieces 9½″ x 3″ and two inside door pieces 9½″ x 3″. Align the inside and outside piece with right sides facing. Add the

batting on top. Sew along three sides of the rectangles, leaving the fourth long side open. Trim seams and turn right side out. Quilt the doors, and then sew them into section 4 by placing them on top of the interior panel.

Three sides of the church are outlined by two borders. The 5″-wide inside border is made up of two white strips, cut 2½″ wide, and one center yellow strip, cut 1½″ wide. The outside border of white crosses on a blue print completes the quilt. (Figure 10.)

As work proceeded by the Landrum club, two separate wall hangings evolved. In addition to the white brick church, a brown brick church was made in secret for a member of the club who had performed services "above and beyond the call of duty." This second quilt had added significance since the recipient's husband was the local minister.

***Here's the Church and Here's the Steeple***
(photograph on page 78)
Finished quilt: 64″ x 50″
Perimeter: 6½ yards (228″)
Fabric requirements:
    Remnants for quilt top: Total of 3 yards
    Backing: 3 yards
Templates: Eight (184 pieces)
    R1 (44)
    R3 (73)
    T9 (12)
    T10 (4)
    T12 (30)
    T19 (8)
    Sp6 (6)
    Sp21 (7)
Cross block on page 91.

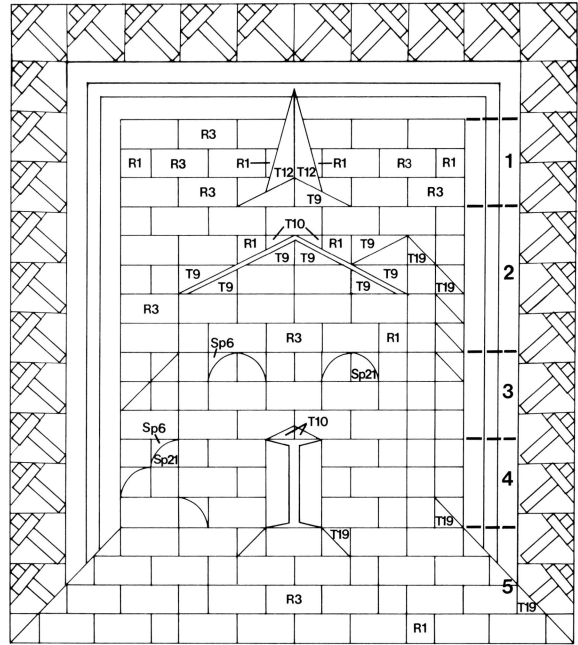

Figure 10

## ADD-A-MEMBER BANNER
(photographs on pages 77, 78, 79)

We originally planned to have picture squares of people framing the church in *Here's the Church and Here's the Steeple.* As the pattern developed on paper, however, we discovered that the people were not in proportion to the church, so we decided to use the people to make a banner. As each member created her own likeness, adding personal touches to the completed square, the *Add-A-Member* banner came to life. This type of banner could be a guild project used to decorate a meeting room or a project for a family celebration.

The figure in the block is based on rectangular piecing. Attach any extra frills on skirt or bodice as the background is added. Embroidery accents complete the face. When adding the hair, use a hoop to help prevent any pulling or take-up in the fabric.

## MORMOR'S QUILT

Grandmothers and quilts seem to go together in any language. This quilt takes its name from the Swedish word for grandmother—*mormor*. Our guild adapted the colorful design for lap quilting.

The beauty of this pattern comes from a contrast of color in the log strips and the use of a large print in the triangles and hexagons.

To make each square, add the 1½"-wide log strips to all four sides of the hexagon in a clockwise direction. Ten strips are added, and then triangles are sewn on opposite corners to complete the 10½" square. Four 10½" squares are combined to form a 20½" block which is then lap-quilted. (*Double Irish Chain* is put together in this same way.) Notice the secondary design that appears once the blocks are joined.

*Mormor's Quilt* (photograph on page 79)
Finished quilt: 80" x 100"
Perimeter: 10 yards (360")
Pieced blocks: Twenty 20" squares (four 10" squares for each block)
Fabric requirements:
    Floral print: 3½ yards
    Log strips: 1 yard each of 3 colors
    Backing: 6 yards

## OFFSET MAPLE LEAF VESTS

Combine maple leaf blocks with the segments you made in the "back door" exercises (Chapter 5) and make a unique quilted vest using your favorite pattern. When arranging and placing these segments, it may be necessary to cut out extra solid shapes. Play with your shapes, testing various combinations. This is a fun project for guild members because, although all the vests are based on the same maple leaf design, they will still be very different since each shows its maker's personality.

Too often I hear the comment, "Oh, I don't want to get involved in a large ladies' group." If everyone had that attitude, think of all the worthwhile clubs and activities that would not have succeeded. Recognize the fact that it takes dedication, tolerance, and a true giving spirit to grow and develop as a group. As in any project, there is a definite correlation between the amount of effort put forth and the amount of fun and satisfaction derived. (And remember, if you don't show up, you'll probably be nominated for an office.)

# Giving Your Best

What better way to give of yourself than to give a gift from your heart made with your hands! With the knowledge you have of quilting, you can make terrific gifts for your family and friends. The projects don't have to be full-size quilts, although I have given directions for a perfect quilt for your favorite teenager. The simpler projects such as totes, belts, and picture frames will also make lovely gifts for Christmas or other occasions.

You can start your decorations ahead of time, too. Begin several months ahead to stitch a tree skirt, a holiday hang-up, or special place mats for Christmas morning.

## DENIM PATCH DELIGHT

Blue jeans are savored for that just-right faded look and then what happens? They are outgrown or out-of-style. Recycle blue jeans and give them new life in a quilt. A quilt stitched from favorite jeans can be a comforting reminder of home to a college student. This quick quilt project is made entirely on the machine and depends on the jeans having raveled and become softer with use.

Cut the legs and trunk of jeans into odd-shaped pieces, all approximately the same size. Save any pockets, unusual patches, fringed bottoms, belt loops, and zippers for special placement on the quilt. Cut any accent fabric you wish to incorporate into odd-shaped pieces as well.

Spread out a bandanna for the block backing and position a square of batting on top. Starting in the center of the block, place the odd-shaped denim pieces in a random setting on top of the batting. Overlap each raw edge at least ¼", and pin the pieces in place. A wonderful collage of various shades of blue emerges as the block develops. Occasionally slip in accent colors to brighten the blue denim.

Match the bobbin thread with the backing and use any suitable thread on top. If you are using decorative machine stitches, a contrasting thread color, such as bright red, is a good choice. Starting in the center of each block, machine-quilt along the loose denim edges, using one stitch or a variety of stitches. Try to have a stitching plan that will allow you to sew continuously, rather than stopping and starting in many places.

After nine blocks are complete, align them with backs together and machine-stitch with a ¼" seam allowance. Sew one row of three blocks together and then attach a second row of three blocks. This lap-quilting connection joins the blocks with one line of stitching, bringing the raw edges to the top. Any fraying is held by the stitching and adds texture to the surface. To complete this *Denim Patch Delight*, attach a contrasting bias strip around the perimeter with a decorative or straight stitch.

*Denim Patch Delight* (photograph on page 82)
Finished quilt: 72" x 72"
Perimeter: 8 yards (288")
Blocks: Nine 24"-square blocks
Backing: Nine 24"-square bandanna handkerchiefs
Fabric requirements:
    Clean, worn, but still sturdy jeans
    Accent fabric such as plaid or bright calico

*Another use for your old jeans—the* Ultimate Tote. *(See page 6.)*

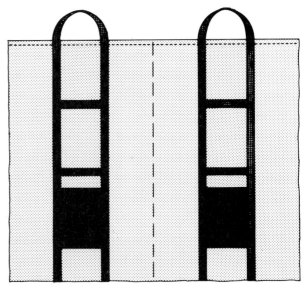

Figure 1

## THE EXPANDING TOTE

This great, easy-to-make, gigantic tote bag can be a laundry bag for the college student or the perfect storage bag for your masterpiece quilt. It just keeps growing as you unfold its three sets of handles.

### Materials
1¼ yards (45″ wide) prequilted fabric
6 yards of binding for the handle

### Method
Cut off 9″ (¼ yard) from the entire length of fabric. From the ¼ yard, cut two 11″ x 9″ rectangles for pockets. Turn the top edge of each rectangle under and machine-stitch a narrow hem. To finish the top of the tote, machine-stitch a narrow hem on one 45″ edge of the remaining large piece. With right sides together, position the bottom edge of the pockets 5″ up from the bottom of the large piece and centered on each side. Sew the bottom edge of the pockets in place and flip upward.

Cut four 9″-long strips of binding for the short handles and divide the remaining binding in half. Pin the short handles to the right side of the fabric above the pockets. Pin the two remaining strips of binding along each side of the pockets and 9″ handles, extending the excess binding at the top to form the long handles. The long strips of binding will overlap the short handles and pockets. Topstitch along each edge of the long strips of binding, securing each short handle and pocket. Top of pocket and short handles are left open and free. (Figure 1.)

Fold the entire bag in half with wrong sides together. Sew sides and bottom with a French seam so that the raw edges will be concealed.

After stitching across the bottom, square off the bottom corners by sewing a triangular tab 3″ from each corner. Turn the bag right side out, and you have a handy tote that can be enlarged or reduced to suit your needs.

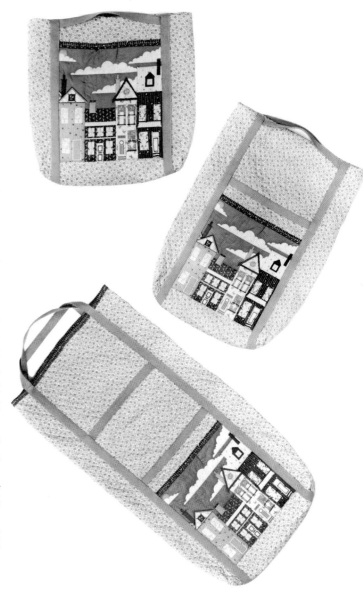

## ROPE BELT (photograph on page 80)

Make this stylish belt for a fashion-conscious friend or to accessorize your own wardrobe. The belt looks great in a holiday plaid or a solid fabric.

### Materials
2 (40″) pieces of bias strip, cut 1½″ wide
2 (45″) pieces of cording
2 (40″) pieces of fat upholstery welting
2 (2½″ x 10½″) pieces of Pellon fleece
2 (5″ x 12″) pieces of fabric
1 (6″) piece of Velcro

### Method
Fold the right sides of the bias strip together. Insert the cording inside the strip, against the fold. Lay the welting on top of the bias strip. (Figure 2.) Sew across one end of the folded bias strip, catching the ends of both the upholstery welting and the cording. Sew with a ¼″ seam allowance on the long raw edge. Be careful not to catch the welting or cording in this seam. Invert the tube by pulling the cording. (A little coaxing is necessary at the beginning.) Cut the tube into two equal lengths. Lay the lengths together and tie a square knot in the center. With seams to the back, machine-stitch the ends of the welting to keep them in place, and hand-tack the square. (Figure 3.)

The back of the belt is made by covering two pieces of Pellon (one with a pointed end) with fabric. Center the two pieces of Pellon on fabric and pin in place. With right sides together, machine-sew the raw ends of the knotted center to each Pellon rectangle. Pull the excess fabric around to cover the back of the Pellon. Form a flat-lapped seam and baste in place. Stitch Velcro in place to create your fastener according to your waist measurement. Machine-quilt lines close together to reinforce the Pellon and catch the Velcro.

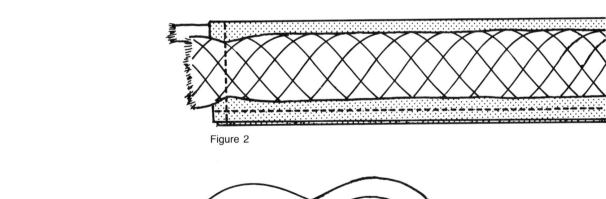

Figure 2

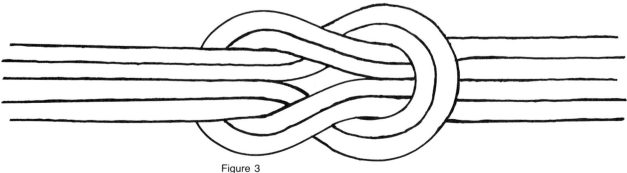

Figure 3

## BASKET LINING AND LID
(photograph on page 79)

Dress up a plain basket with a soft layering of fabric, and you have the perfect container in which to present your homemade jams and jellies, cookies, and other goodies. You'll be giving two gifts—the goodies and the basket.

### Materials
Prequilted or a single layer of fabric. The amount needed depends on the size of your basket.
1 yard of ribbon

### Method
Any shape basket can be properly lined if you make a pattern based on these measurements. First, measure around the basket top from the center of one end to the center of the other end. Add ¼″ to each end for seam allowances. (Figure 4.) Second, measure from the top of the rim around the outside of the basket to the center of the bottom of the basket. (Figure 5.) Add to this measurement the desired amount of overhang, usually 1¼″ for large baskets and 1″ for smaller baskets.

Based on these measurements, draw a rectangular pattern piece. Mark a fold line across the bottom of the pattern, and cut a notch for the handle equal to the depth of the overhang. (Figure 6.)

### Lining
Trace your pattern on folded fabric and cut out your basket lining. Fold the right sides of the fabric together, aligning the notches, and sew one end. With a ¼″ seam allowance, attach an eyelet trim or a ruffle between the notches around the top of the lining, with right sides together and raw edges aligned. Now sew the lining and the ruffle at the other end. Refold the lining so that you form a flat triangle at each end. (Figure 7.) With the seams centered, pin the triangles in place. Check to make certain

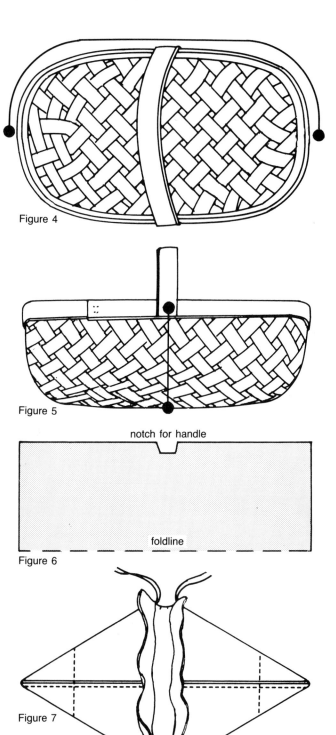

Figure 4

Figure 5

notch for handle

foldline

Figure 6

Figure 7

that the lining fits the basket. Before you stitch, make any needed adjustments by repinning the triangles.

Cut the ribbon into four 9″-long pieces and, with a zigzag stitch, attach them to the sides of each notch. A zigzag stitch can also be used to finish the raw edges of the notched area.

## Lid

A lid provides a finished look to your basket, and it's a great way to show off your piecework. Make your favorite 12″-square block, but leave an opening in the center for a handle, and you have a lid for your basket. To determine the lid area, measure across the top of the basket in both directions. Depending on the size of your basket, the 12″-square block may need an extra row of piecework or a border added.

Cut a facing the same size as your block, with a slit in the center for the handle. To finish the opening, align the right sides of the facing and pieced block. Machine-stitch around the opening; clip corners and invert. Raw edges can be finished by turning ¼″ of the outside edges to the inside and stitching.

## SOFT FRAMES (photographs on pages 27 and 84)

A fabric insert containing vital facts, such as the names, date, inspiration, dedication, or any special techniques used in the making of your quilt will be a treasured memento in years to come. Preserve these in a soft frame made from the remnants of your quilt. The soft frame is also a good way to display a favorite photo, and making the frame yourself allows you to coordinate it with your own decorating scheme.

## Materials

Heavy mat board or mounting board (found at an office supply store)
Small amount of batting
2 (3″ x 9″) strips of fabric
2 (3″ x 11″) strips of fabric
1 (11″ x 9″) piece of facing fabric
1 (13″ x 11″) piece of backing fabric
1 (6″ x 8″) piece of fabric for the insert
Small amount of Velcro

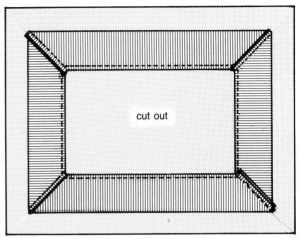

Figure 8

## Method

On the back of one edge of one 11″ strip of fabric, make a mark 2½″ from each end. Draw a diagonal line to the nearest corner on the opposite edge. Place this strip on top of a 9″ strip, right sides together. Sew on the diagonal line to form a mitered corner. (Backstitch to reinforce.) Repeat for the other two strips. Then join the two pairs of strips to form a frame. Center the front of the frame on the facing with right sides together. Sew around the opening with a ¼″ seam. Cut out the 4″ x 6″ opening, clipping each corner. (Figure 8.)

Turn the fabrics right side out and press open. Trim the outside edges of the facing so that they align with the front. Cut your board into two pieces: one 10″ x 8″ piece with a 6″ x 4″ inside opening, and one 10″ x 8″ piece with no center opening.

Position the batting on the front of the mat board frame and glue in place. If you are going to have a fabric insert, stitch Velcro to four corners of the facing to hold the insert. Attach the other side of the Velcro to the insert after your message is typed. (Cross-stitching your message on hardanger fabric can be an alternative to typing.)

Insert the cardboard with batting between the fabric frame and facing. Stack the 13″ x 11″ backing fabric right side down, the 10″ x 8″ mat board, and the front of the frame. Roll the backing fabric to the front around the unfinished edge. Trim the excess fabric from the corners. After pinning in place, use a zipper-foot attachment and stitch in place.

## PATCHWORK WELCOME BANNER
(photograph in Introduction)

It seems I see triangles and parallelograms in rooftops and windows everywhere. Translating these geometric shapes to patchwork is a natural way to develop buildings and houses for quilting. Use the block Home, Pieced Home as a pillow top or create a group of patchwork pictures to hang over your mantel (photographs on pages 81 and 83). Or make a welcome banner for your foyer.

### Materials
1 (12") Seldom Inn block
1 (3½" x 11") rectangular piece of fabric
1 mailbox and post (cut 3 extra R5)
6 (4½" square) Maple Leaf blocks
3 (2" x 3 yard) strips of different fabrics
1 yard of backing

### Method
Machine-piece all of the Seldom Inn block together except the bottom row. To form a mailbox, align the short end of the two extra R5s with right sides together and stitch at one short end. Turn right side out and place it over R5, finished edge on the left, in the bottom right-hand corner of the bottom row. Attach this row to the rest of the block. Sew the mailbox post to the end of the large rectangle. Sew this entire piece to the block.

Sew the three strips of fabric together to form a striped band 5" x 3 yards. Cut two 15" lengths and two 12" lengths from the band. Attach the 12" lengths to the block, one to the top and one to the bottom. Sew the Maple Leaf blocks to the ends of the 15" bands, and then sew these bands to the sides of the block, to complete the 21" x 24" pieced top. Cut the backing and batting 21" x 24" also. Baste all three layers together (top, batting, backing).

To prepare the loops to hang your banner, cut four 10" lengths from the pieced band. Cut the batting and backing for these pieces 5" x 10".

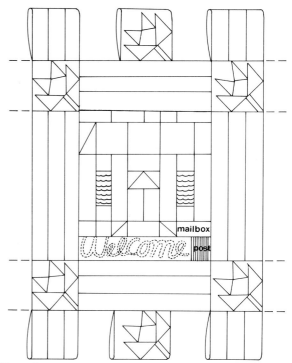

Figure 9

Sew the three layers on both sides and invert. Quilt each band. Fold in half, wrong sides together, and align raw edges with the raw edges at each outside corner. (Figure 9.) To prepare the Maple Leaf center loops, sew a rectangle of coordinating fabric to each of the remaining two Maple Leaf blocks to make them 10" long. Make these loops as you did the others.

Align the right sides of the top of banner and backing on top of the batting. Machine-stitch these layers together with the batting against the feed dogs. Leave a 6" opening on one side; trim seam allowances and invert. Whipstitch the opening closed; baste and quilt from the center outward.

## HOLIDAY HANG-UP (photographs on pages 80 and 83)

Gather together a bunch of quilted leaves to decorate your door or mantel for the holidays. Make the oak leaves for your Thanksgiving celebration or holly leaves for Christmas.

### Materials
1 yard of green fabric for holly leaves or brown
    fabric for oak leaves or assorted scraps
Batting
Fabric for backing
Pattern pieces on pages 122 and 123

## Method

Trace around the leaf pattern A21 or A25. Pin the batting underneath each leaf and machine-stitch all the way around, leaving a 2″ to 3″ opening. (The batting should be against the feed dogs.) At each inside turn of a leaf, make one right-angle stitch on the machine to ease the turn when the leaf is inverted. After sewing, trim each leaf very close to the inside right angles. Turn right side out and hand-sew the opening closed. Topstitch a vein down the middle of each leaf using a decorative stitch or straight stitch. After preparing the backing piece (A9) as you did the leaves, machine-stitch all the leaves but one in place. Tack the top leaf to hide the machine stitching securing the other leaves. Red buttons or red pom-poms from curtain fringe make pretty berries. A wide bow at the top—6½″ wide and about 30″ long—completes your hang-up.

### DRESDEN CHRISTMAS TREE SKIRT
(photograph on page 81)

A circular, pieced skirt with a delightful surprise—it's reversible! Use it on your table and then, during the holiday season, turn it over and use it as a tree skirt.

### Materials
2½ yards of fabric (divide amount by number and colors of fabrics used)
Lightweight batting
1 (10″ x 20″) piece of lightweight plastic or cardboard for template

### Method
To make your template, draw a straight line 20″ long. At one end of this line, draw a perpendicular line 9″ long, with the midpoint at the 20″ line. At the other end of the 20″ line, draw a 1¼″ perpendicular line with its midpoint at the 20″ line. Connect the endpoints of the perpendicular lines. (Figure 10.) Add a ¼″ seam allowance on all sides and grainline.

Using your template, cut out 16 pieces for the front and 16 pieces for the back. Fold all 32 cut pieces in half lengthwise with right sides together. To make the triangular points, sew a ¼″ seam across the wide end, and another across the narrow end, backstitching each time. (Figure 11.) Trim off the right angle and turn right side out; press into an equal triangle at each end. This is the same technique we used to make the points on the Grandmother's Fan block in the quilt, *Gypsy in My Soul*.

Cut out 16 pieces of batting. The batting is the same size as the segment without the triangular points at the end. (Figure 12.)

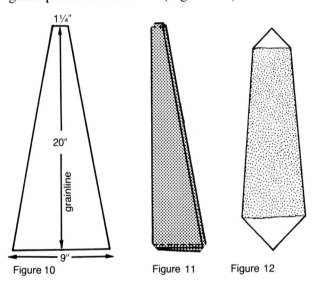

Figure 10          Figure 11          Figure 12

Begin the skirt by stacking one segment from the back and one from the front, right sides together. Place the batting underneath against the feed dogs and sew with a ¼″ seam allowance. Turn right side out. Continue to add segments one at a time using the stack-and-sew method. Be sure to line up your triangular points. The final segment will need a finished outside edge.

Draw a line around the outside and inside edges of the skirt at the base of the triangular points. Sew a decorative stitch to secure these loose, finished ends and to catch the edge of your batting.

## YOU'RE AN ANGEL PLACE MATS
(photograph on page 80)

What more festive touch than angel place mats at that special holiday party? Based on triangles with an appliqué face, the place mats can be rectangular or square.

**Materials** (for one place mat)
12″ x 19″ rectangular piece of fabric or 19″ x 19″ square
12½″ square Angel block
2 (4″ x 12½″) borders for the rectangular place mat
4 (4″ x 20″) borders for the square place mat
1 (12½″ x 20″) piece of backing and Pellon fleece for the rectangular place mat
1 (20″ square) piece of backing and Pellon fleece for the square place mat
See block, page 90, for pattern pieces.

### Method
Construct one Angel block and check the size with your 12″ master block. Attach the borders. Add borders to two sides for a rectangular place mat, or for a different look, add four mitered borders and create a square place mat with a triangular overhang.

Stack the block and backing, right sides together. With the batting against the feed dogs, sew around all four sides, leaving a 3″ opening to invert your fabric. Turn the place mat right side out and whipstitch the opening closed. Baste the place mat and either hand-quilt or machine-quilt the three layers. You might add a quilted halo for a finishing touch. Corners may be curved if desired.

### ROUND TREE BLOCK PILLOW (photograph on page 81)

The Round Tree block makes an attractive Christmas pillow when made in red and green fabric. Use other favorite blocks to make additional pillows.

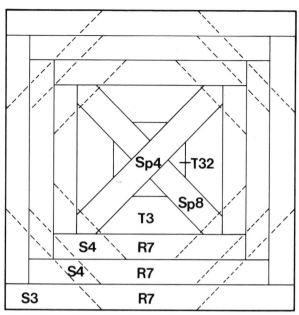

Figure 13

**Materials**
Small amount of white fabric and black fabric
4 (4″) squares of green fabric
8 (3″) squares of green fabric
3½″ yards of red fabric (cut 1½″ wide)
½ yard of border fabric for border and backing
See block, page 92, for pattern pieces.

### Method
Start in the center by sewing and flipping the small triangle T32 to the corner of the large triangle T3. Sew two of these pieced triangles to either side of Sp8. Form the center square by attaching these two large triangles to the sides of Sp4. Add four red log cabin strips (1½″ wide) in a continuous manner around the four sides of the center square. (Figure 13.)

Before sewing the second row of strips, fold four 3″ green squares into triangles and place them in each corner of the block. The folded edge of each triangle should face the inside of the block. Sew the second row of strips, securing the raw edges of the corner "trees" at the same time. Place four more trees in the corners, and add the final row of strips.

For the trees at the outside corners, fold the four 4″ green squares into triangles and sew in the top corners, overlapping the log cabin strips and other trees. Complete the block with mitered borders and a white double-bias ruffle.

At Mary's Island, *a 56″ x 38″ wall hanging made for a husband's office, represents geese seen in early morning light. Try your hand at quick-piecing the five flying geese bands using T34 and T31. (See page 41, Chapter 5.)*

**Below:** *The Landrum Library Quilters stand hand in hand. Each member added special touches to create a quilted self-portrait in our Add-a-Member Banner.*

Here's the Church and Here's the Steeple; *open the door and see all the ...quilting. A white brick church stands proudly atop the steps and is surrounded by a border of crosses.*

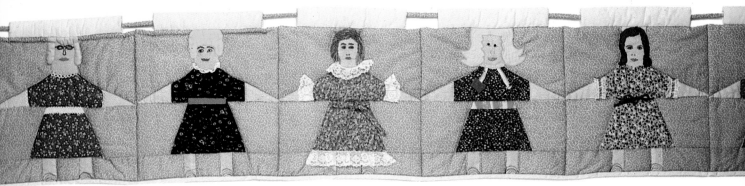

**Right:** *A tisket, a tasket, it's a lined, ruffled basket. Completing the set is a patchwork lid made from the Bow Basket block.*

Mormor's Quilt *finally shows us a way to incorporate a large floral print into pieced blocks for lap quilting.*

**Left:** *Continuous curves create the mini-landscapes on two cummerbunds, and taffeta takes on a new twist in the rope belt.*

**Below:** *Say "good morning" to Christmas with these adorable* You're an Angel *place mats. A holly leaf banner complements the setting.*

**Left:** *Use the Round Tree and Home, Pieced Home block or choose another favorite block to create pillows that accent your decor.*

**Below:** *A reversible* Dresden Delight *tree skirt and an expandable tote are easy projects for the busy quilter's Christmas.*

**Left:** *Recycled blue jeans are combined with a touch of plaid fabric and bandannas in Denim Patch Delight. The odd shapes of denim are secured in place with many novelty machine stitches.*

**Right:** *All the indispensable tools of the trade can be packed in one tote— the perfect sewing studio for the quilter on the move.*

**Below:** *Geometric shapes are interpreted as, left to right, Rock of Ages, Possum Trot, Cozy Cottage, and Old MacDonald's Farm. They all look quite at home hanging over a rustic mantel topped by a bunch of quilted oak leaves.*

83

# Designs & Patterns

The patchwork and appliqué block designs presented here are arranged in three categories—Beginner, Intermediate, and Advanced. The shading in each block is only a suggestion. You might achieve a completely different look by switching the positions of the dark and light-colored fabrics. The broken lines extending from each of these designs show how the sections of the blocks are put together.

Listed beneath each design are the pattern pieces used. The number in parentheses tells you how many of each piece you will need.

The patterns appear in the next section of this chapter, except for some of the very small appliqué pieces used in the patchwork blocks. All the shapes are full-size and include seam allowances and grainlines.

Below many of the blocks are smaller blocks illustrating one way in which that design may be quilted. Stencils used for some of these designs are included in this chapter following the patterns. Don't feel limited to these designs, however. They are merely ideas with which you can experiment. Just try to keep the amount of quilting consistent in each block of your quilt.

## *BEGINNER*

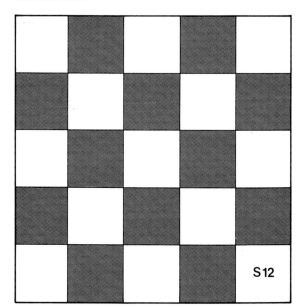

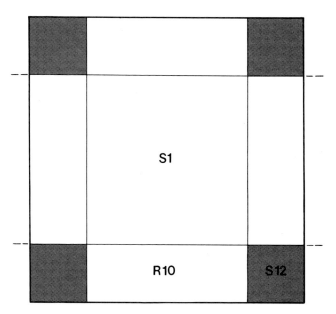

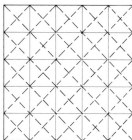

**Irish Chain (A)**
10″ Block
1 template; 25 pieces

S12 (25)

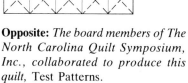

**Opposite:** *The board members of The North Carolina Quilt Symposium, Inc., collaborated to produce this quilt,* Test Patterns.

**Irish Chain (B)**
10″ Block
3 templates; 9 pieces

S1 (1)     R10 (4)
S12 (4)

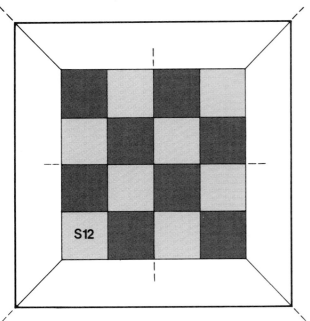

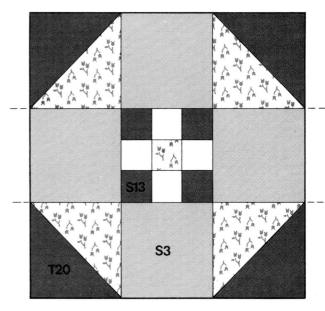

### Rescued 16 Patch
12″ Block
1 template; 16 pieces

S12 (16)
2″-wide mitered
borders

### Shoo Fly Variation
12″ Block
3 templates; 21 pieces

S3 (4)
S13 (9)
T20 (8) grainline #1

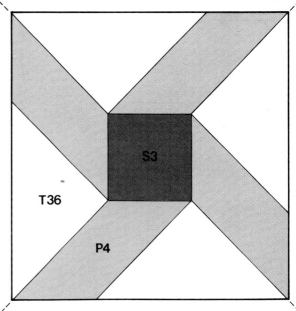

### Test Pattern
16″ Block
3 templates; 40 pieces

S12 (36)
T20 (2) grainline #1
P2 (2)

### Formal Garden
12″ Block
3 templates; 9 pieces

S3 (1)      P4 (4)
T36 (4)

*(Special piecing instructions on page 64.)*

86    *Beginner*

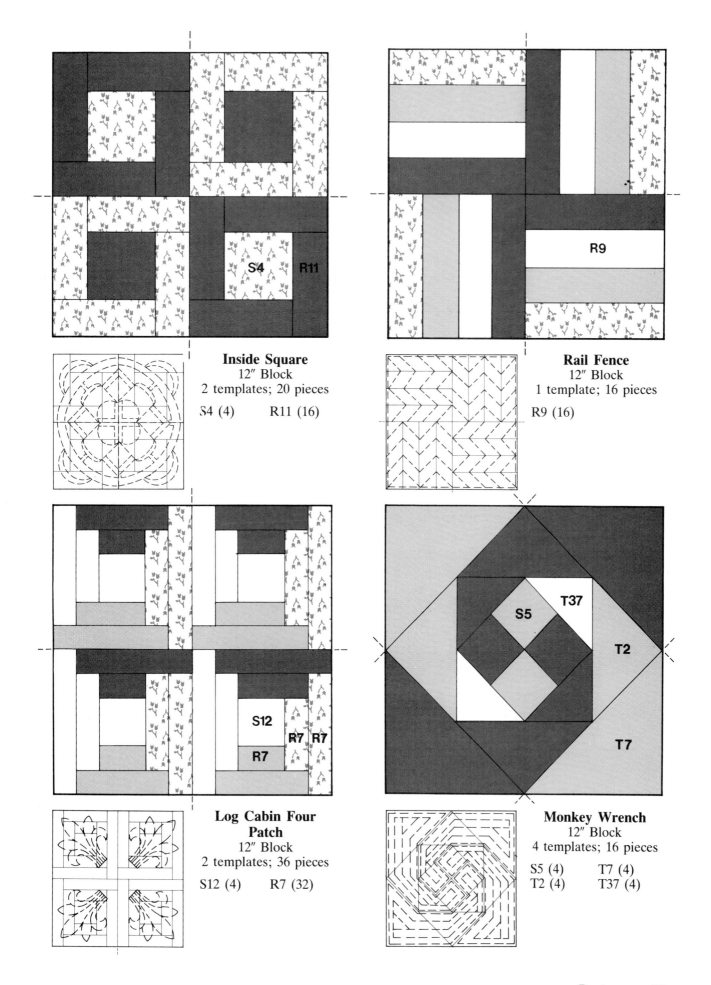

**Inside Square**
12″ Block
2 templates; 20 pieces

S4 (4)　　　R11 (16)

**Rail Fence**
12″ Block
1 template; 16 pieces

R9 (16)

**Log Cabin Four Patch**
12″ Block
2 templates; 36 pieces

S12 (4)　　　R7 (32)

**Monkey Wrench**
12″ Block
4 templates; 16 pieces

S5 (4)　　　T7 (4)
T2 (4)　　　T37 (4)

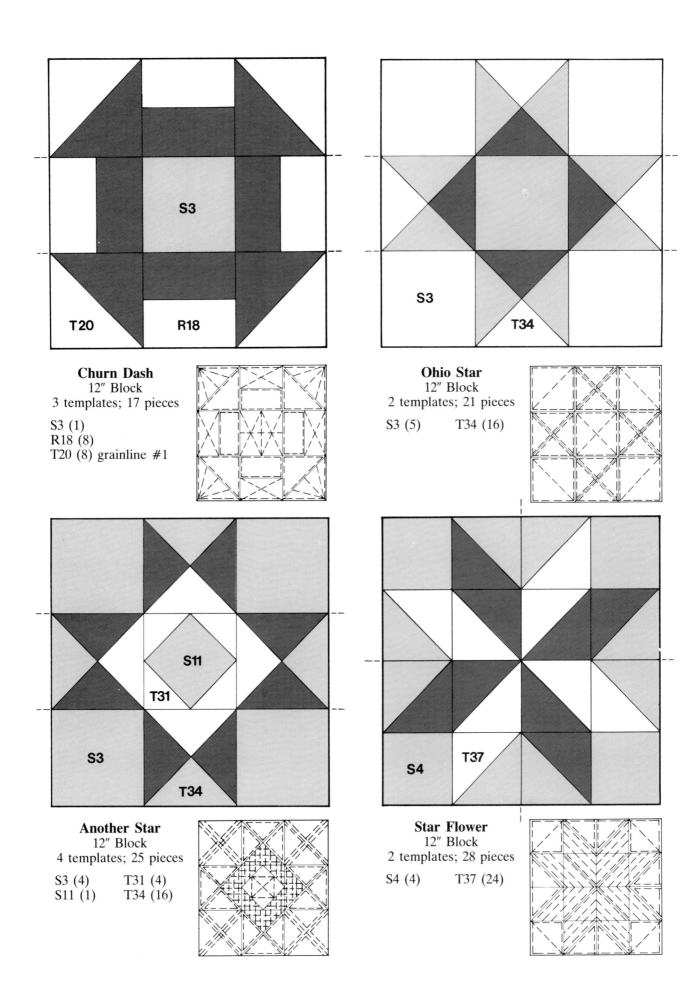

**Churn Dash**
12″ Block
3 templates; 17 pieces

S3 (1)
R18 (8)
T20 (8) grainline #1

**Ohio Star**
12″ Block
2 templates; 21 pieces

S3 (5)    T34 (16)

**Another Star**
12″ Block
4 templates; 25 pieces

S3 (4)    T31 (4)
S11 (1)   T34 (16)

**Star Flower**
12″ Block
2 templates; 28 pieces

S4 (4)    T37 (24)

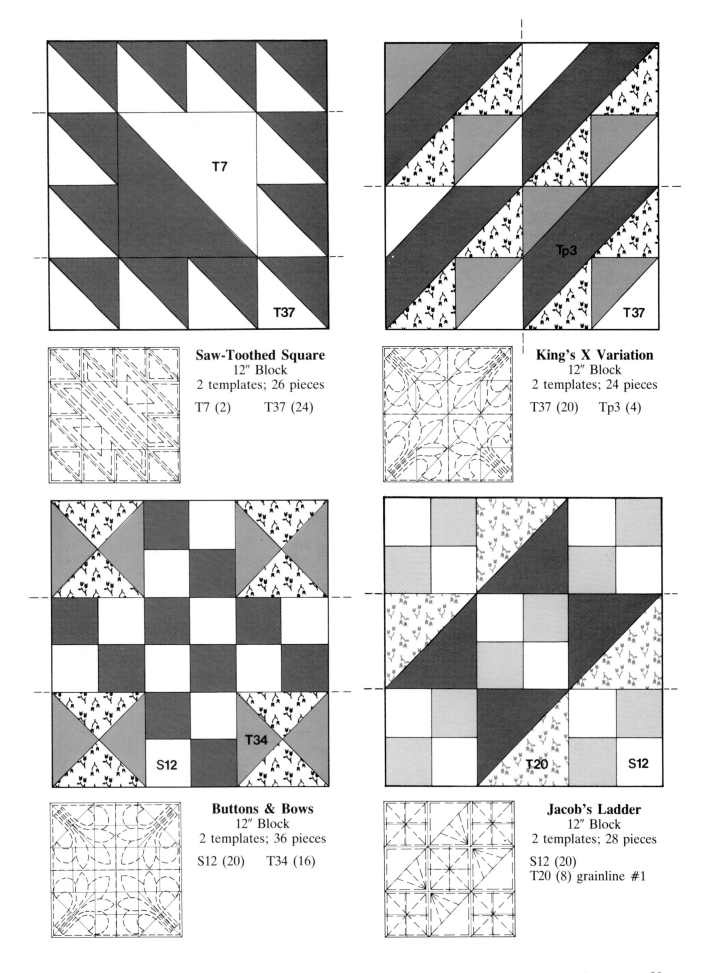

**Saw-Toothed Square**
12″ Block
2 templates; 26 pieces

T7 (2)     T37 (24)

**King's X Variation**
12″ Block
2 templates; 24 pieces

T37 (20)     Tp3 (4)

**Buttons & Bows**
12″ Block
2 templates; 36 pieces

S12 (20)     T34 (16)

**Jacob's Ladder**
12″ Block
2 templates; 28 pieces

S12 (20)
T20 (8) grainline #1

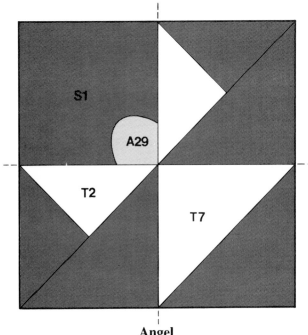

**Angel**
12″ Block
4 templates; 10 pieces

S1 (1)      T7 (4)
T2 (4)      A29 (1)

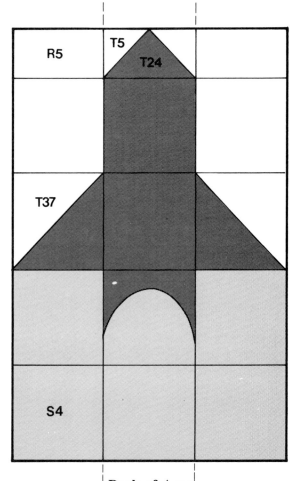

**Rock of Ages**
9″ x 13½″ Block
5 templates; 20 pieces

S4 (10)     T5 (2)
R5 (2)      T37 (4)
T24 (1) grainline #1
appliqué arch

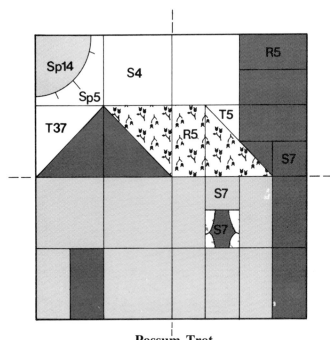

**Possum Trot**
12″ Block
7 templates; 30 pieces

S4 (5)      T37 (5)
S7 (3)      Sp5 (1)
R5 (13)     Sp14 (1)
T5 (2)
appliqué curtains

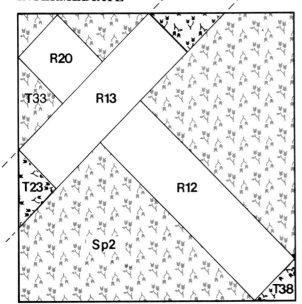

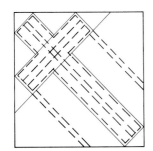

**Cross**
5″ Block
7 templates; 11 pieces

R12 (1)    T38 (2)
R13 (1)    T33 (2)
R20 (1)    Sp2 (2)
T23 (2)

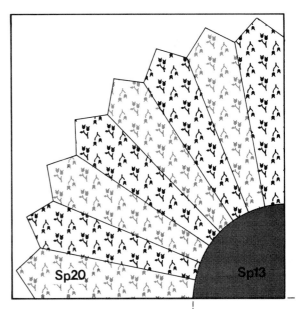

**Home, Pieced Home
Variation**
12″ x 15″ Block
6 templates; 58 pieces

S7 (6)     R11 (5)
R5 (14)    T5 (24)
R9 (1)     T13 (8)
1½″ x 10½″ strip

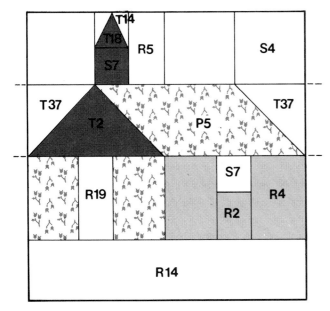

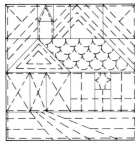

**Church on a Hill**
12″ Block
12 templates; 20
pieces

S4 (3)     R19 (1)
S7 (2)     T2 (1)
R2 (1)     T14 (2)
R4 (4)     T18 (1)
R5 (1)     T37 (2)
R14 (1)    P5 (1)

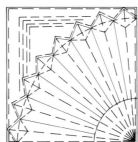

**Grandmother's Fan**
12″ Block
2 templates; 9 pieces

Sp13 (1)    Sp20 (8)
12″-square foundation

*(Special piecing instructions on page 75.)*

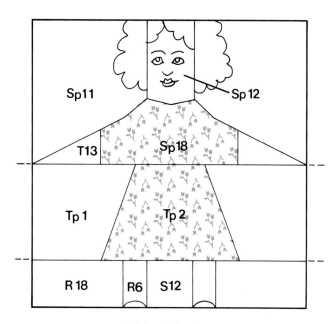

### Add-a-Member
12″ Block
9 templates; 14 pieces

S12 (1)     Tp2 (1)
R6 (2)      Sp11 (2)
R18 (2)     Sp12 (1)
T13 (2)     Sp18 (1)
Tp1 (2)
embroider features

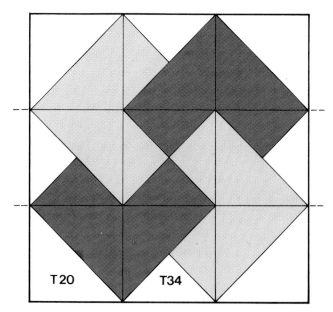

### Card Tricks
12″ Block
2 templates; 24 pieces

T20 (12) grainline #1
T34 (12)

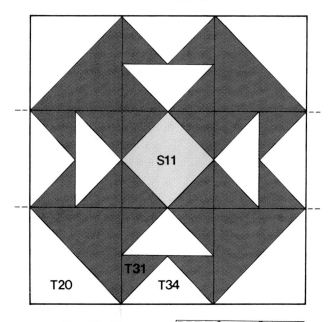

### Double T
12″ Block
4 templates; 37 pieces

S11 (1)
T20 (8) grainline #1
T31 (20)
T34 (8)

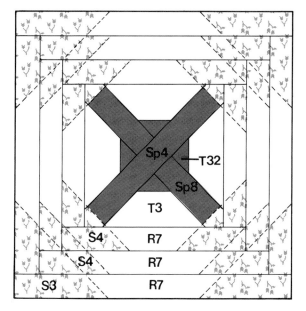

### Round Tree
12″ Block
7 templates; 35 pieces

S3 (4) folded   T32 (4)
S4 (8) folded   Sp4 (1)
R7 (12)         Sp8 (2)
T3 (4)

*(Special piecing instructions on page 76.)*

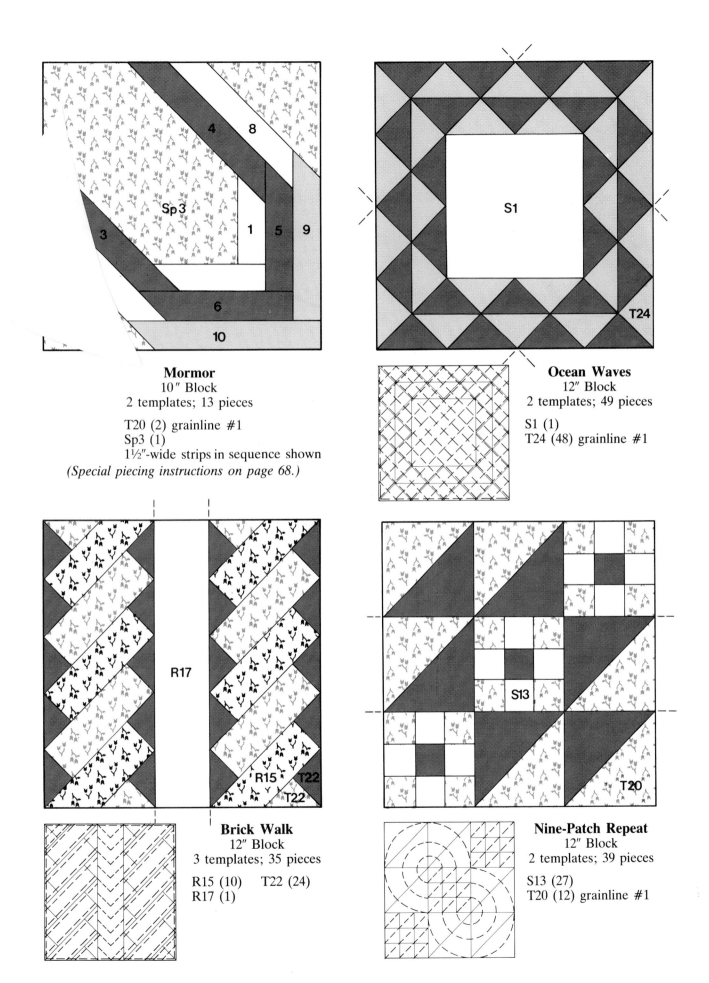

**Mormor**
10″ Block
2 templates; 13 pieces

T20 (2) grainline #1
Sp3 (1)
1½″-wide strips in sequence shown
*(Special piecing instructions on page 68.)*

**Ocean Waves**
12″ Block
2 templates; 49 pieces

S1 (1)
T24 (48) grainline #1

**Brick Walk**
12″ Block
3 templates; 35 pieces

R15 (10)     T22 (24)
R17 (1)

**Nine-Patch Repeat**
12″ Block
2 templates; 39 pieces

S13 (27)
T20 (12) grainline #1

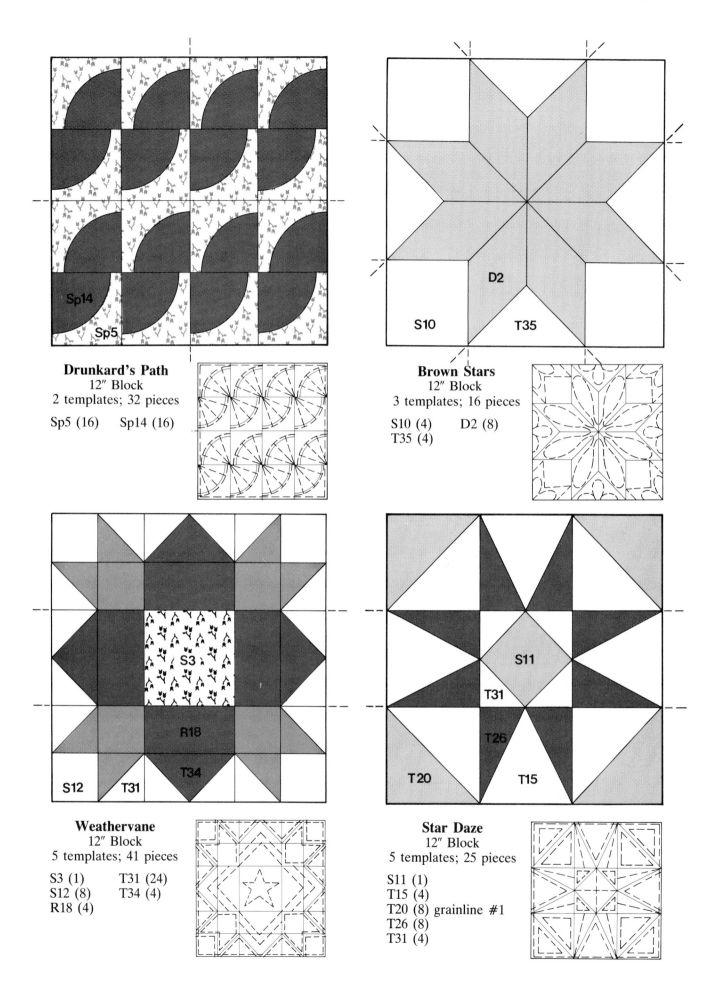

**Drunkard's Path**
12″ Block
2 templates; 32 pieces

Sp5 (16)    Sp14 (16)

**Brown Stars**
12″ Block
3 templates; 16 pieces

S10 (4)    D2 (8)
T35 (4)

**Weathervane**
12″ Block
5 templates; 41 pieces

S3 (1)     T31 (24)
S12 (8)    T34 (4)
R18 (4)

**Star Daze**
12″ Block
5 templates; 25 pieces

S11 (1)
T15 (4)
T20 (8) grainline #1
T26 (8)
T31 (4)

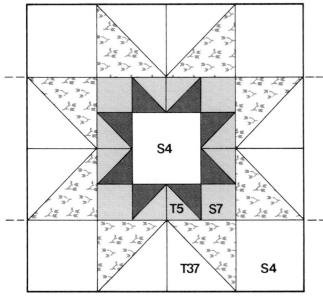

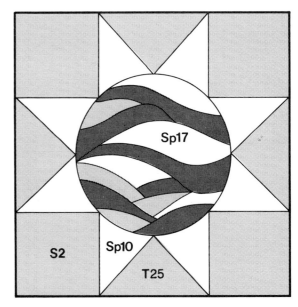

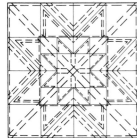

### Double Star Flower
*12″ Block*
4 templates; 41 pieces

S4 (5)          T5 (16)
S7 (4)          T37 (16)

### Stars Over the Smokies
*16″ Block*
4 templates; 17 pieces

S2 (4)          Sp10 (8)
T25 (4)         Sp17 (1)

*(Special piecing instructions on page 53.)*

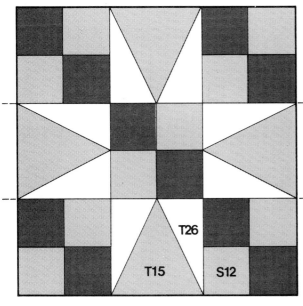

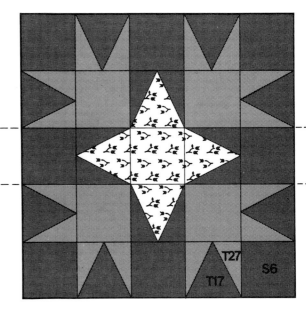

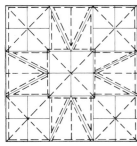

### Fifty-four Forty or Fight
*12″ Block*
3 templates; 32 pieces

S12 (20)        T26 (8)
T15 (4)

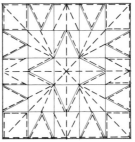

### Glow Shine
*12″ Block*
3 templates; 49 pieces

S6 (13)          T27 (24)
T17 (12)

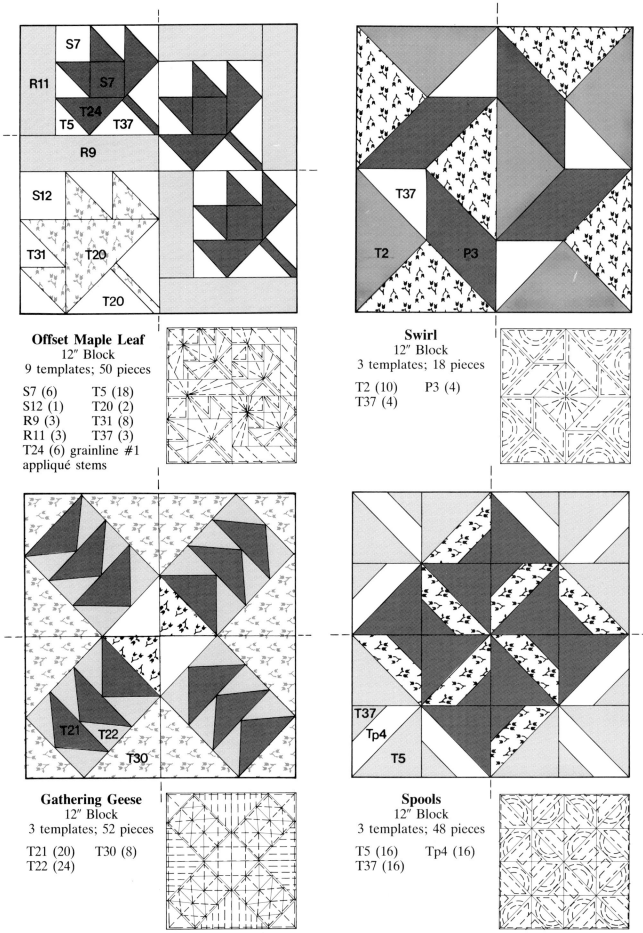

### Offset Maple Leaf
12″ Block
9 templates; 50 pieces

| | |
|---|---|
| S7 (6) | T5 (18) |
| S12 (1) | T20 (2) |
| R9 (3) | T31 (8) |
| R11 (3) | T37 (3) |

T24 (6) grainline #1
appliqué stems

### Swirl
12″ Block
3 templates; 18 pieces

| | |
|---|---|
| T2 (10) | P3 (4) |
| T37 (4) | |

### Gathering Geese
12″ Block
3 templates; 52 pieces

| | |
|---|---|
| T21 (20) | T30 (8) |
| T22 (24) | |

### Spools
12″ Block
3 templates; 48 pieces

| | |
|---|---|
| T5 (16) | Tp4 (16) |
| T37 (16) | |

*(Special piecing instructions on page 41.)*

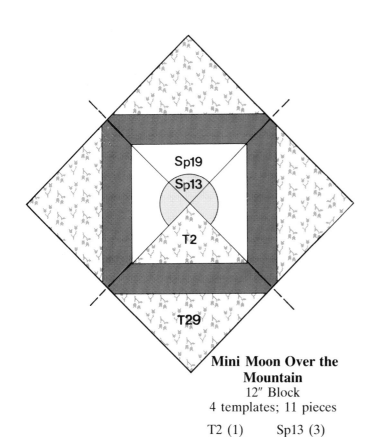

**Mini Moon Over the Mountain**
12″ Block
4 templates; 11 pieces

T2 (1)      Sp13 (3)
T29 (4)     Sp19 (3)
2″-wide mitered
borders

**Lottie's Lily**
12″ Block
4 templates; 50 pieces

S12 (23)    T31 (10)
T5 (16)     Tp6 (1)
appliqué stems

*ADVANCED*

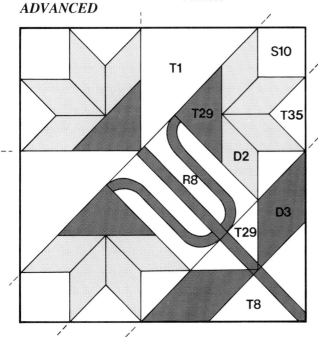

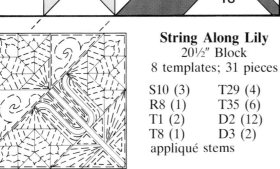

**String Along Lily**
20½″ Block
8 templates; 31 pieces

S10 (3)     T29 (4)
R8 (1)      T35 (6)
T1 (2)      D2 (12)
T8 (1)      D3 (2)
appliqué stems

*(Special piecing instructions on page 62.)*

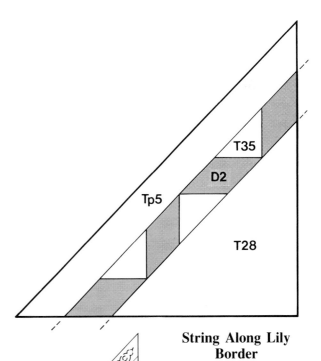

**String Along Lily Border**
20½″ x 20½″ x 29″
Triangle
4 templates; 9 pieces

T28 (1)     Tp5 (1)
T35 (3)     D2 (4)

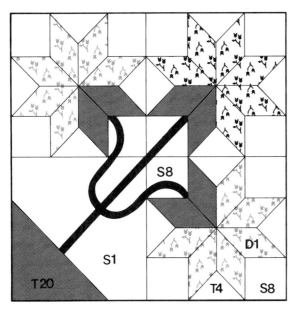

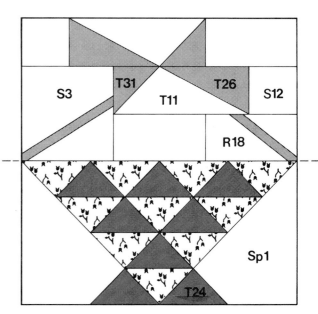

## Mini-Lily
12″ Block
5 templates; 50 pieces

S1 (1)       T4 (12)
S8 (12)      D1 (24)
T20 (1) grainline #1
appliqué stems

## Bow Basket
12″ Block
8 templates; 32 pieces

S3 (1)       T11 (2)
S12 (2)      T26 (2)
R18 (3)      T31 (2)
             Sp1 (2)
T24 (18) grainline #1
appliqué handle

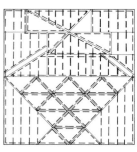

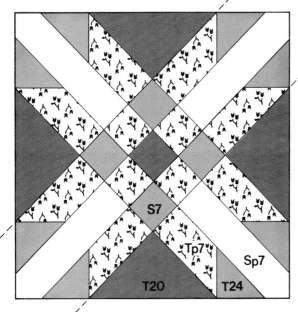

## Mexican Star
12″ Block
5 templates; 33 pieces

S7 (9)
T20 (4) grainline #2
T24 (8) grainline #2
Tp7 (8)
Sp7 (4)

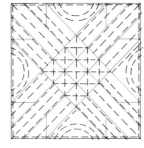

## Rainbow Row
12″ Block
11 templates; 43 pieces

S4 (1)       R16 (6)
S7 (1)       T5 (4)
S9 (4)       T13 (2)
R5 (4)       T16 (1)
             T37 (3)
T24 (1) grainline #1
R7 (16) to fill in
around windows and
doors

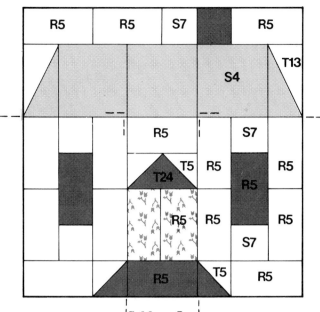

**Seldom Inn**
12″ Block
6 templates; 39 pieces

S4 (3)      R5 (19)
S7 (6)      T5 (6)
            T13 (4)
T24 (1) grainline #1

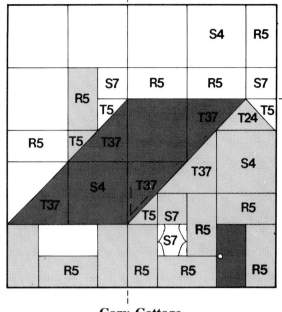

**Cozy Cottage**
13½″ Block
6 templates; 38 pieces

S4 (8)      R5 (15)
S7 (4)      T5 (4)
            T37 (6)
T24 (1) grainline #1
appliqué curtains

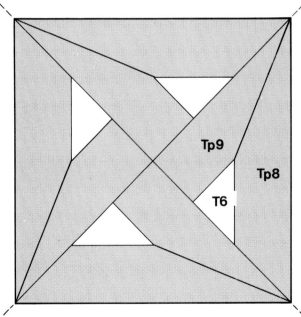

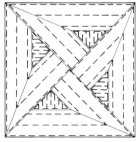

**Shadow Dance**
12″ Block
3 templates; 12 pieces

T6 (4) grainline #2
Tp8 (4)
Tp9 (4)

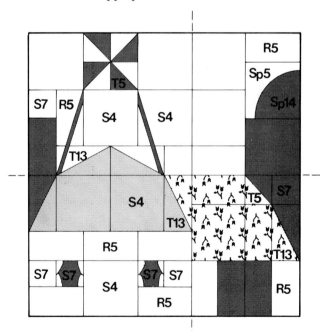

**Old MacDonald's
Farm**
15″ Block
7 templates; 55 pieces

S4 (11)     T13 (10)
S7 (7)      Sp5 (1)
R5 (15)     Sp14 (1)
T5 (10)
appliqué curtains and
windmill posts

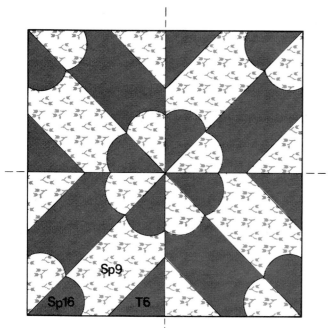

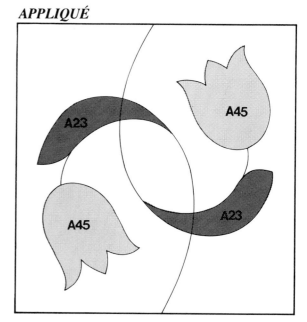

**Virginia's Choice**
12″ Block
3 templates; 32 pieces

T6 (8) grainline #1
Sp9 (8)      Sp16 (16)

**Tulips & Bluebells**
10″ Foundation Block
2 templates; 4 pieces

A23 (2)      A45 (2)

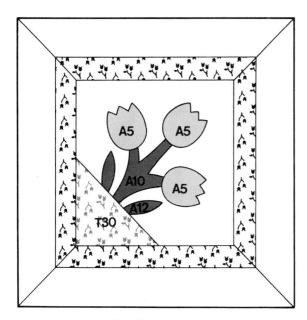

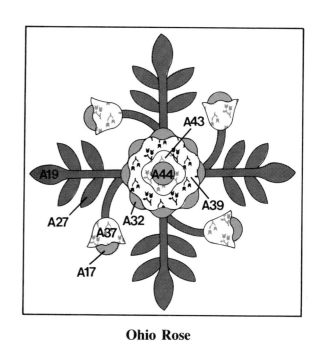

**Tri-State Tulip**
14″ Block
4 templates; 7 pieces

T30 (1)      A10 (1)
A5 (3)       A12 (2)
8″-square foundation
1″-wide inside borders
2″-wide outside borders

**Ohio Rose**
12″ Foundation Block
8 templates; 32 pieces

A17 (4)      A37 (4)
A19 (4)      A39 (1)
A27 (16)     A43 (1)
A32 (1)      A44 (1)
½″-wide bias strips
for curved stems

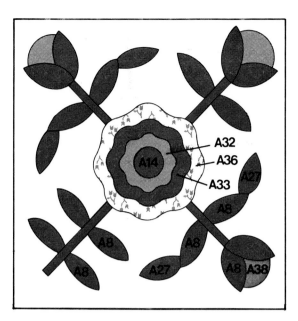

**Rose of Sharon**
12″ Foundation Block
7 templates; 27 pieces

A8 (16)    A33 (1)
A14 (1)    A36 (1)
A27 (4)    A38 (3)
A32 (1)
½″-wide bias strips
for stems

**Great-Grandmother's
Rose**
12″ Foundation Block
4 templates; 13 pieces

A3 (1)    A11 (4)
A4 (4)    A31 (4)

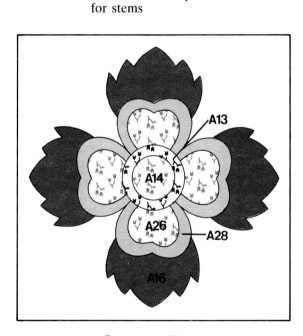

**Lancaster Rose**
12″ Foundation Block
5 templates; 14 pieces

A13 (1)    A26 (4)
A14 (1)    A28 (4)
A16 (4)

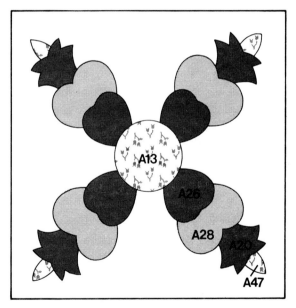

**Radical Rose**
12″ Foundation Block
5 templates; 17 pieces

A13 (1)    A28 (4)
A20 (4)    A47 (4)
A26 (4)

**President's Wreath**
12″ Foundation Block
5 templates; 48 pieces

A14 (4)      A39 (4)
A24 (8)      A41 (8)
A27 (24)
½″-wide bias strips
for stems

**Whig Rose**
12″ Foundation Block
7 templates; 51 pieces

A15 (4)      A39 (1)
A33 (1)      A40 (8)
A35 (16)     A46 (20)
A36 (1)
½″-wide bias strips
for stems

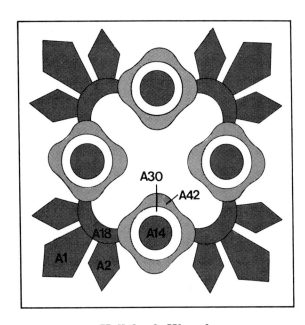

**Hollyhock Wreath**
12″ Foundation Block
6 templates; 28 pieces

A1 (4)       A18 (4)
A2 (8)       A30 (4)
A14 (4)      A42 (4)

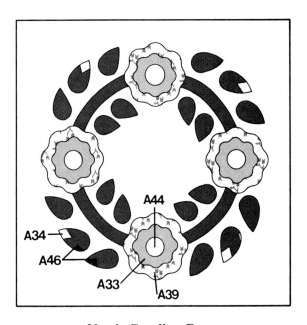

**North Carolina Rose**
12″ Foundation Block
5 templates; 36 pieces

A33 (4)      A44 (4)
A34 (4)      A46 (20)
A39 (4)
½″-wide bias strips
for stems

# Squares

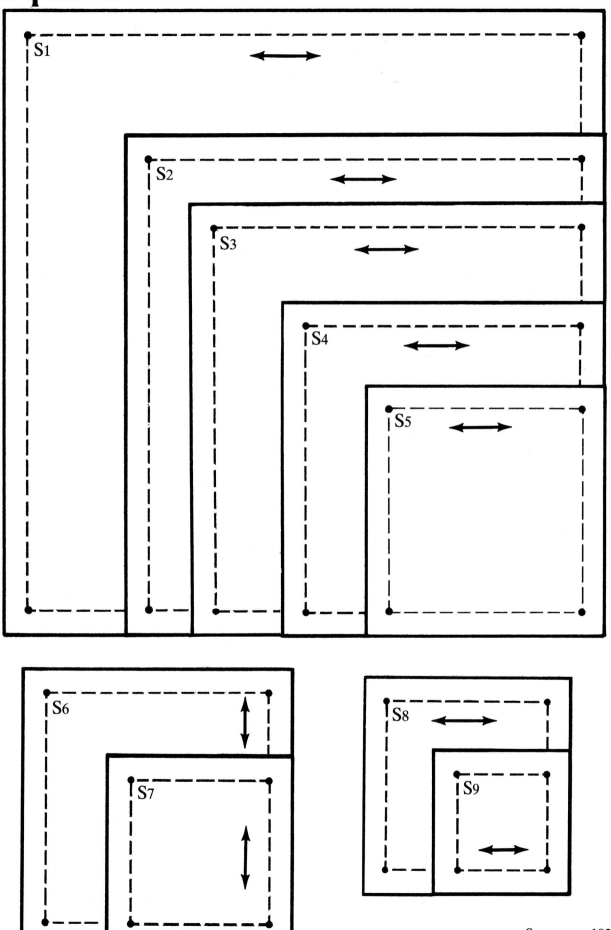

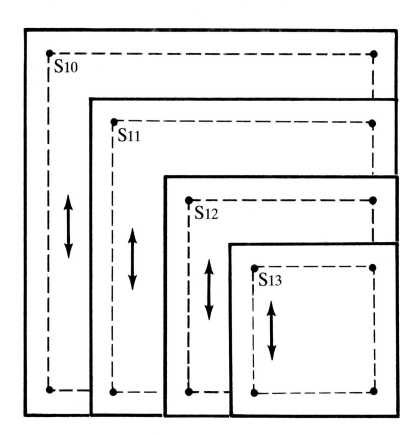

# Rectangles

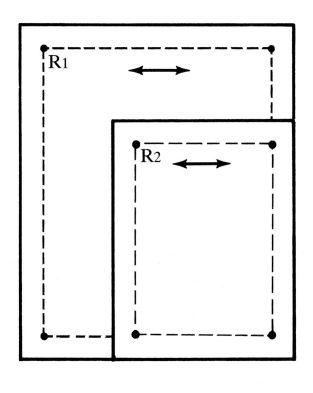

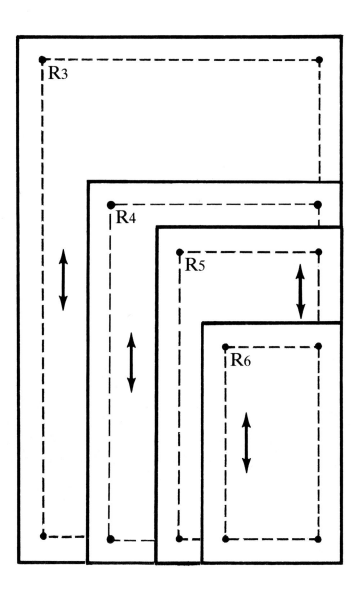

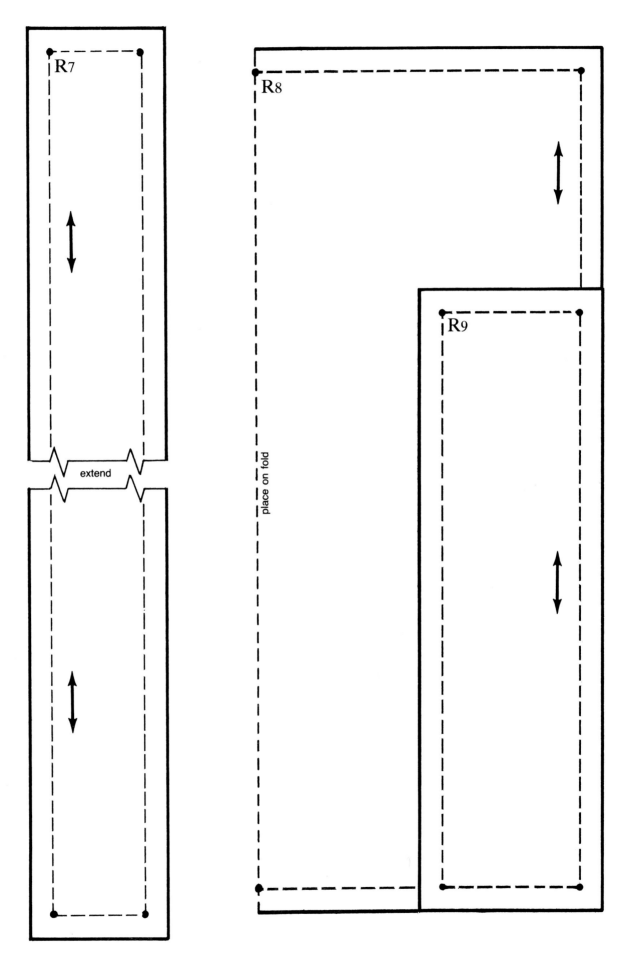

R7

extend

R8

place on fold

R9

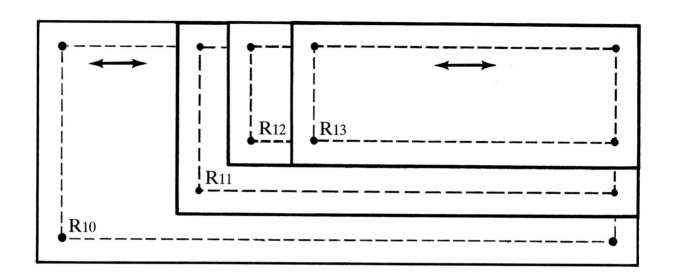

R12
R13
R11
R10

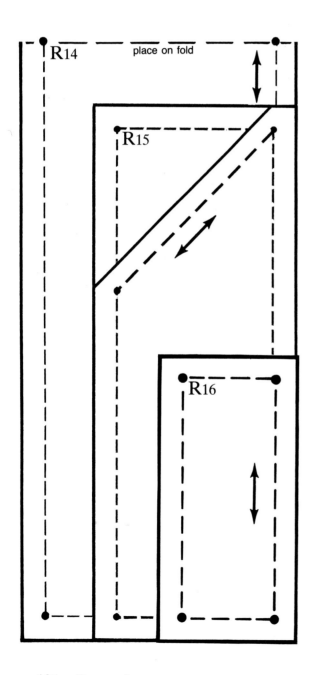

R14 place on fold
R15
R16

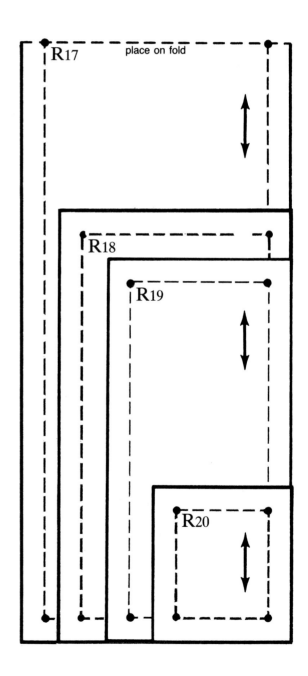

R17 place on fold
R18
R19
R20

# Triangles

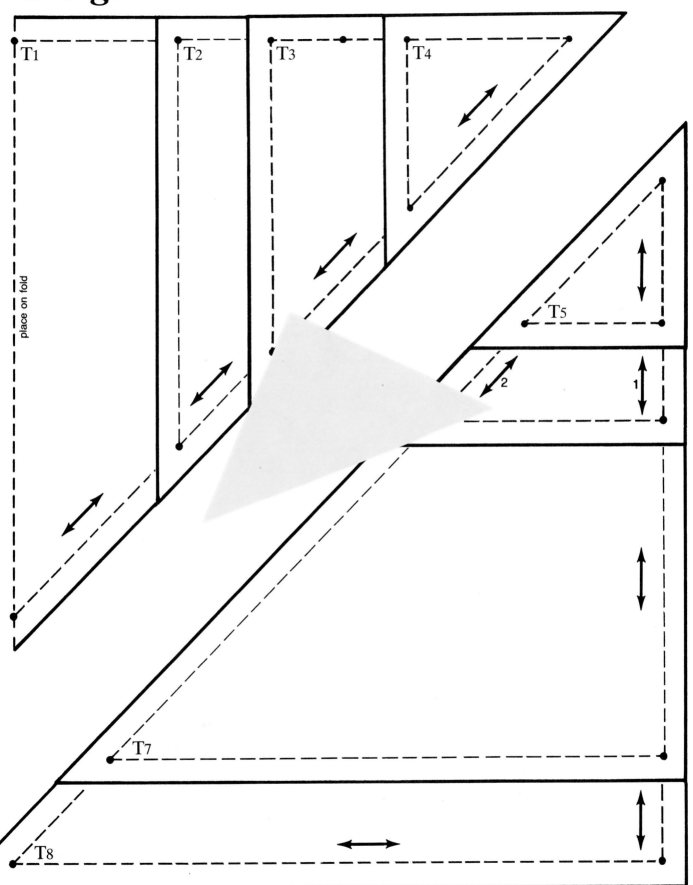

place on fold

T1

T2

T3

T4

T5

T7

T8

1

2

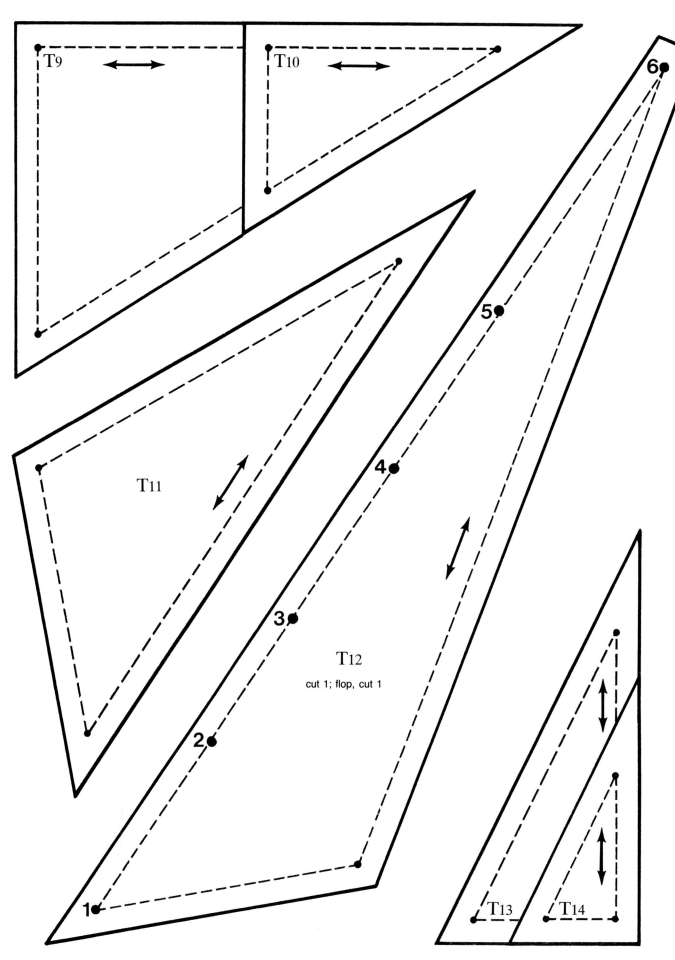

T9

T10

T11

T12

cut 1; flop, cut 1

T13  T14

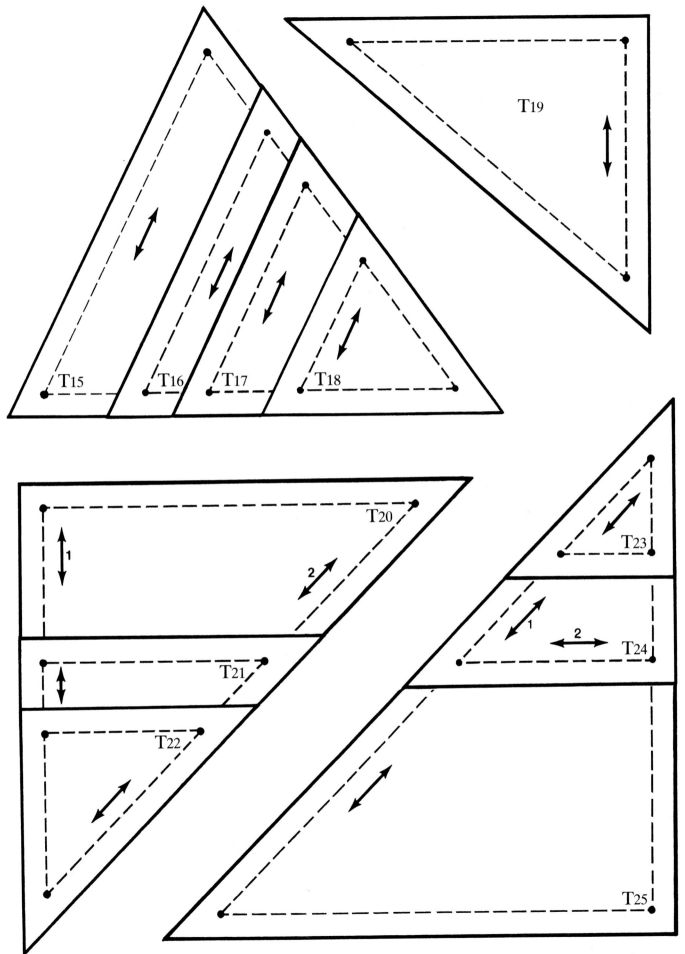

T19

T15 T16 T17 T18

T20
1
2

T21

T22

T23

1
2
T24

T25

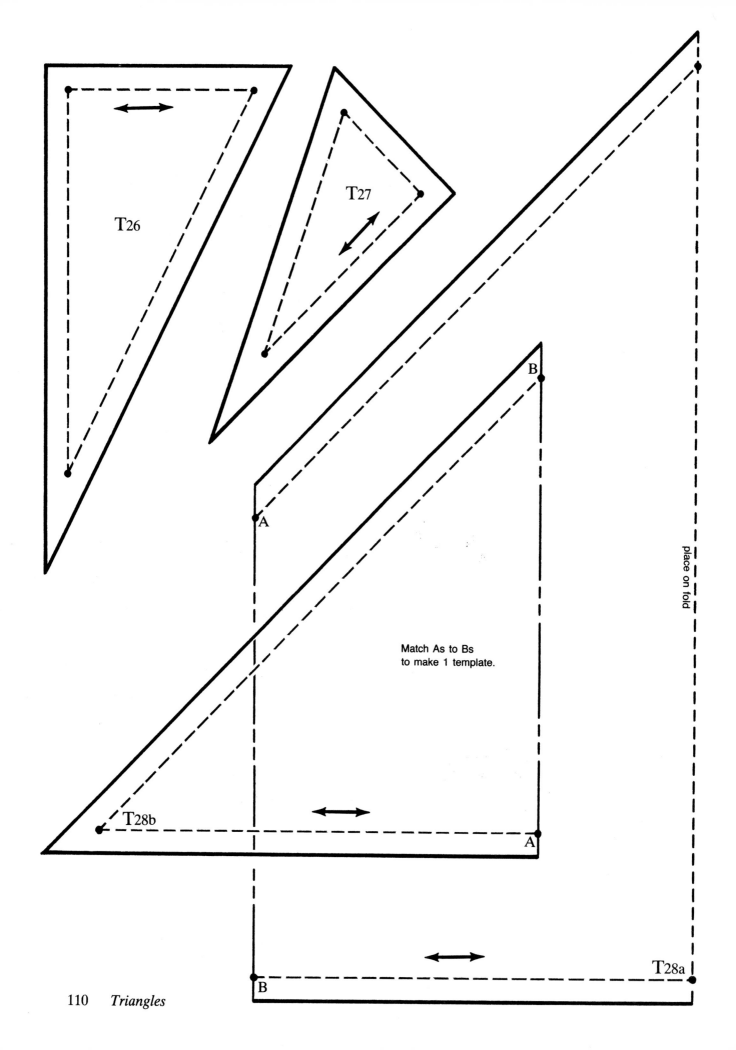

T26

T27

B

A

Match As to Bs
to make 1 template.

place on fold

T28b

A

T28a

B

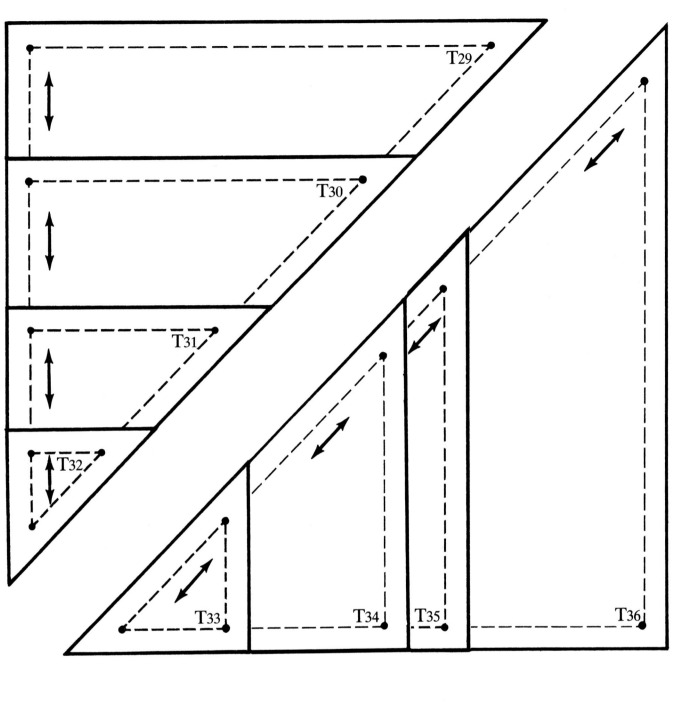

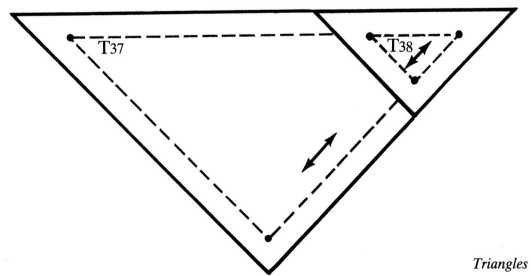

# Parallelograms

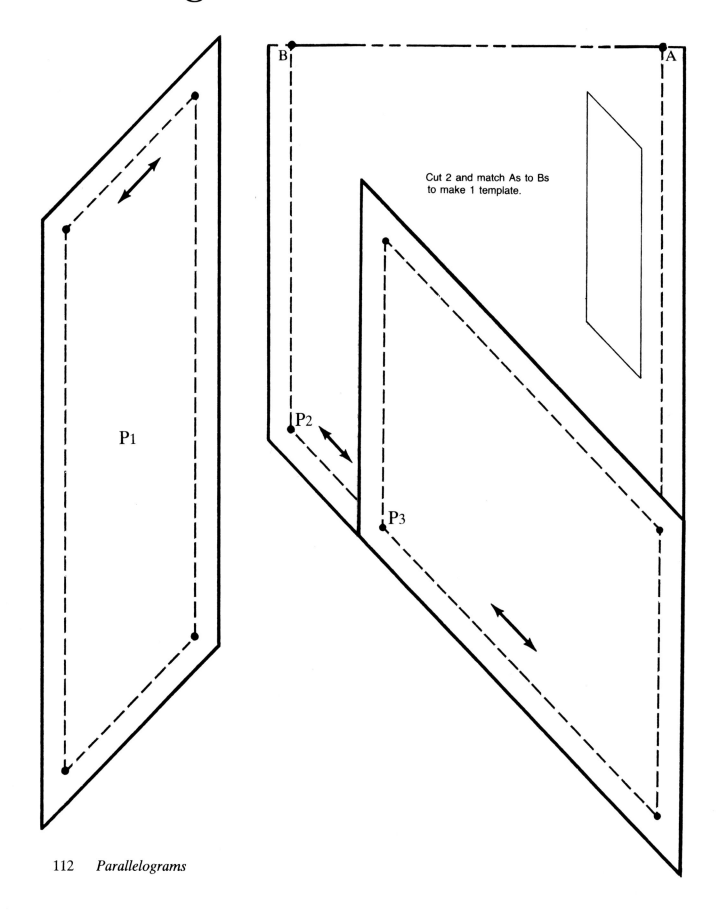

B

A

Cut 2 and match As to Bs
to make 1 template.

P1

P2

P3

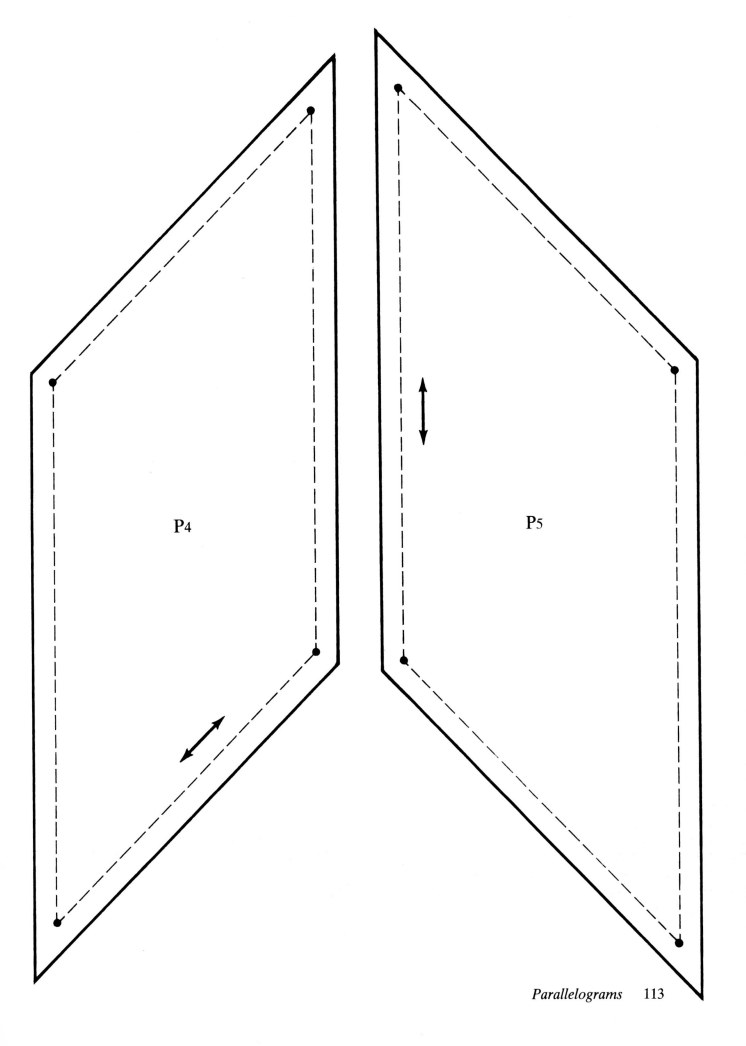

P4

P5

# Trapezoids

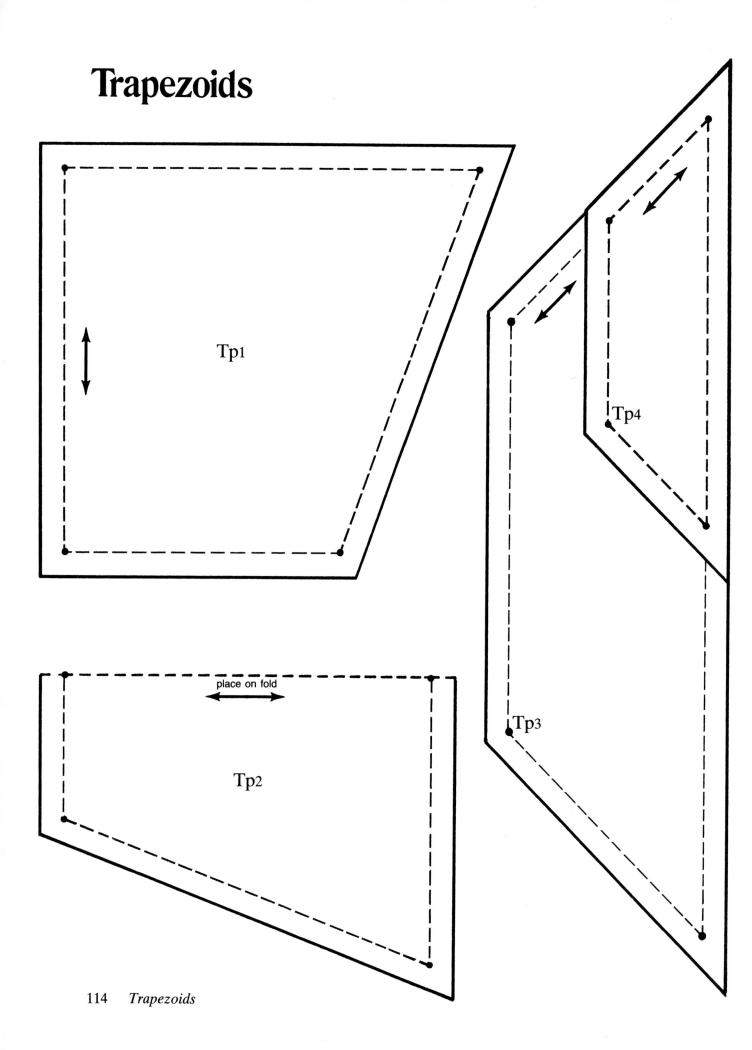

Tp1

Tp2

place on fold

Tp4

Tp3

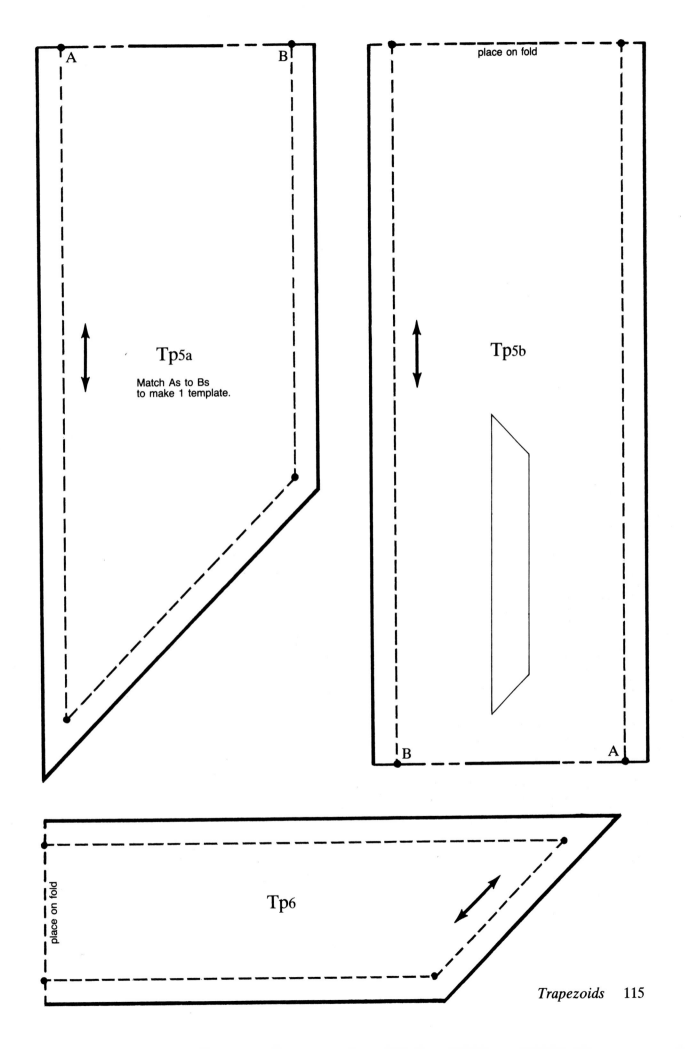

A

B

Tp5a

Match As to Bs
to make 1 template.

place on fold

Tp5b

B

A

place on fold

Tp6

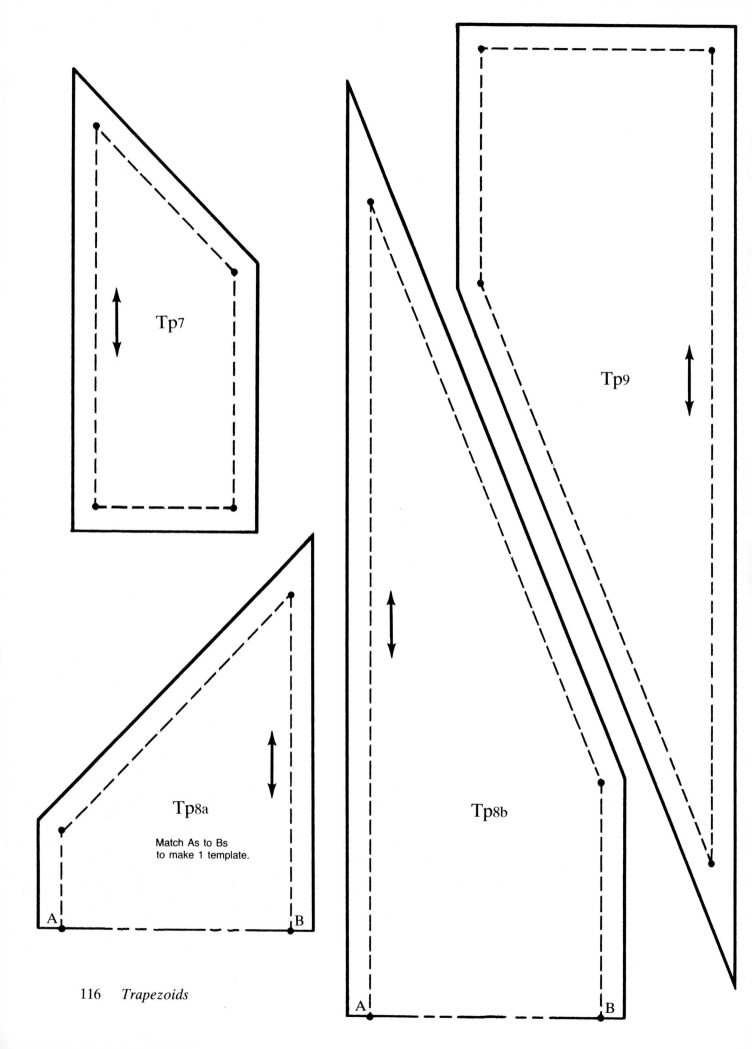

Tp7

Tp9

Tp8a

Match As to Bs
to make 1 template.

A

B

Tp8b

A

B

# Diamonds

## Special Pieces

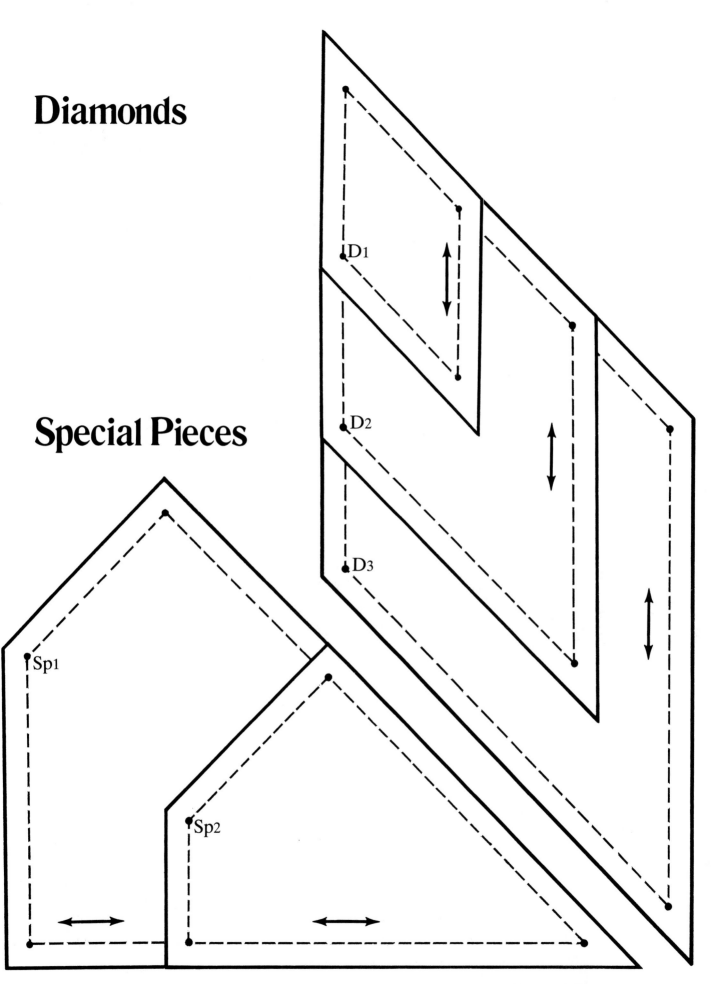

D1

D2

D3

Sp1

Sp2

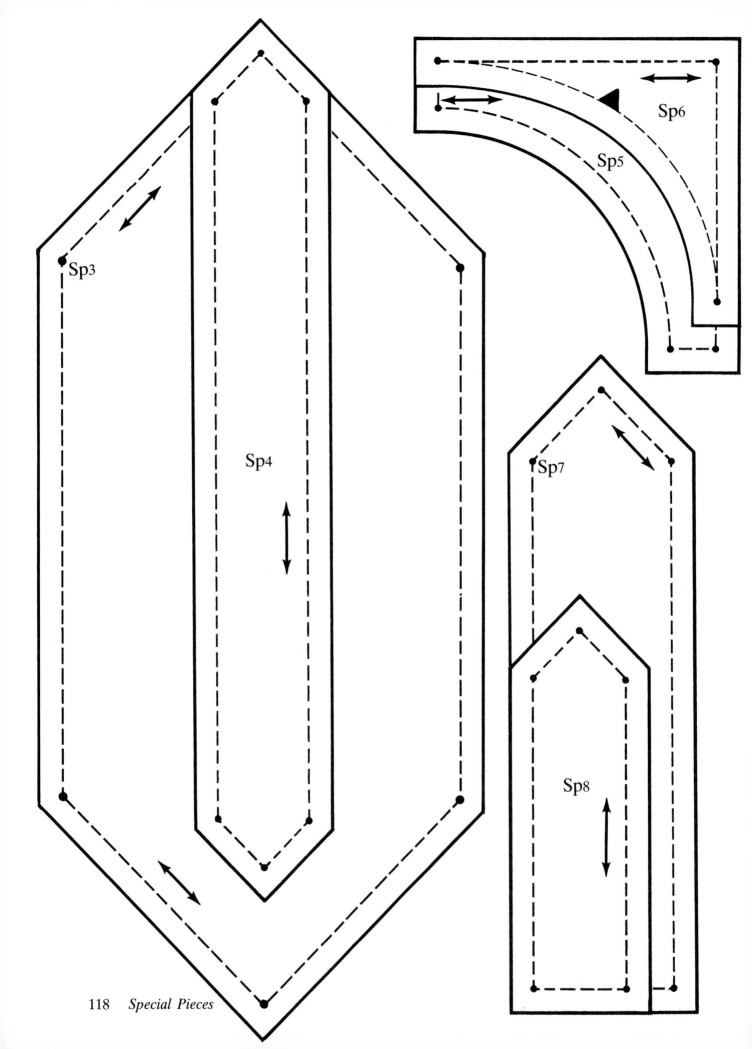

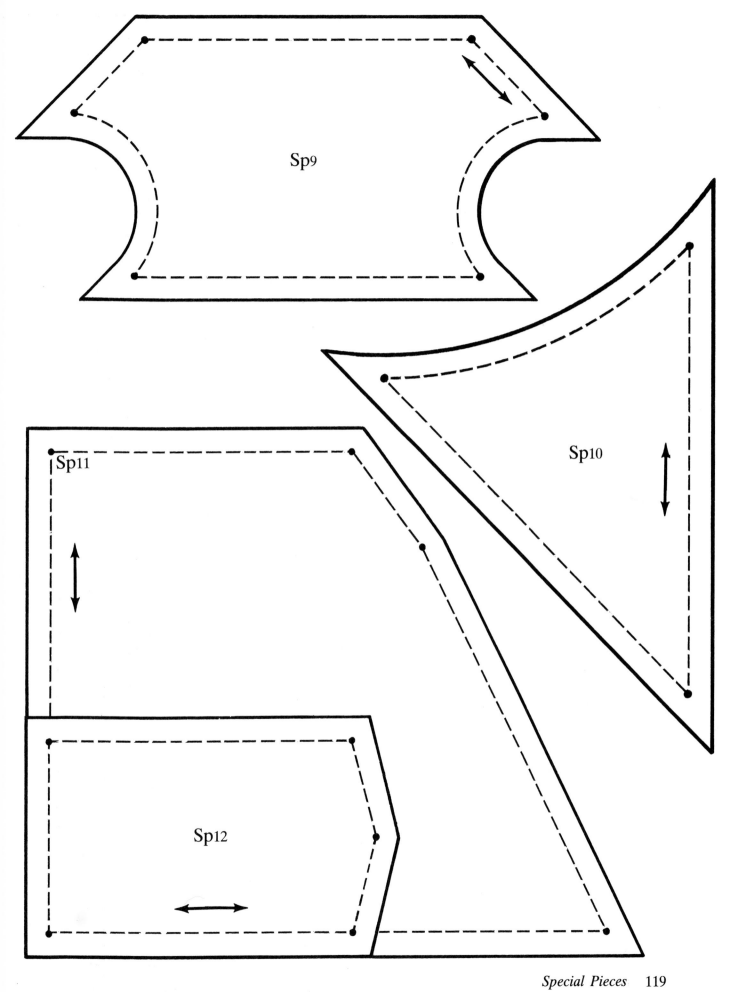

Sp9

Sp10

Sp11

Sp12

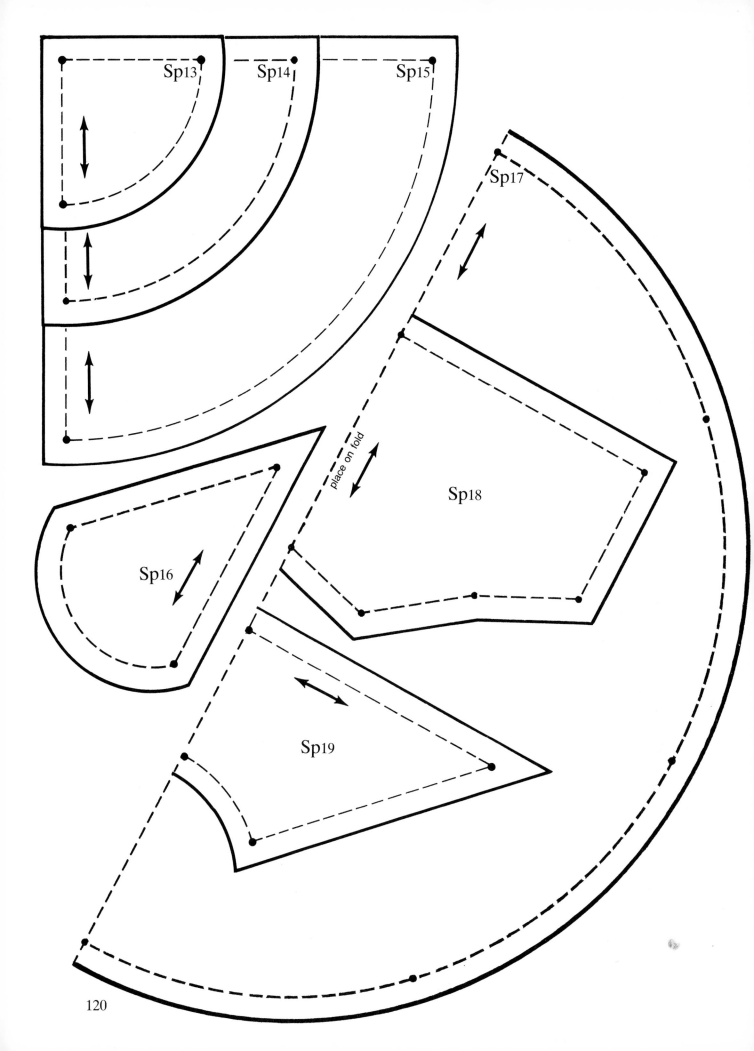

Sp13

Sp14

Sp15

Sp17

place on fold

Sp18

Sp16

Sp19

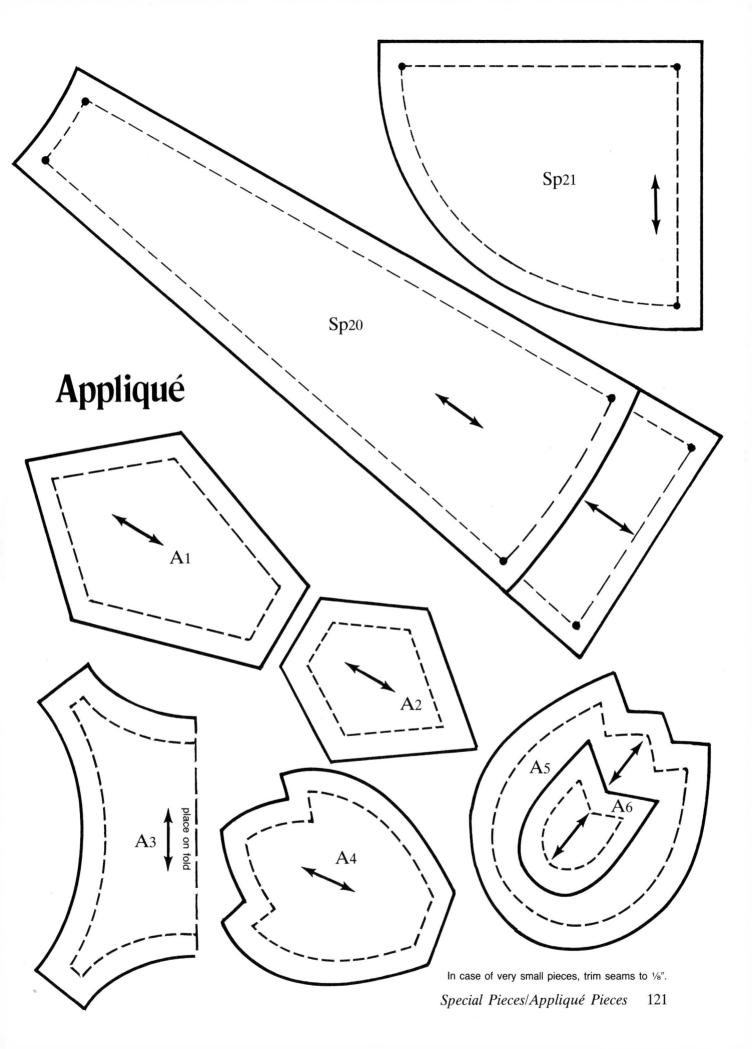

# Appliqué

Sp21

Sp20

A1

A2

A3

place on fold

A4

A5

A6

In case of very small pieces, trim seams to ⅛".

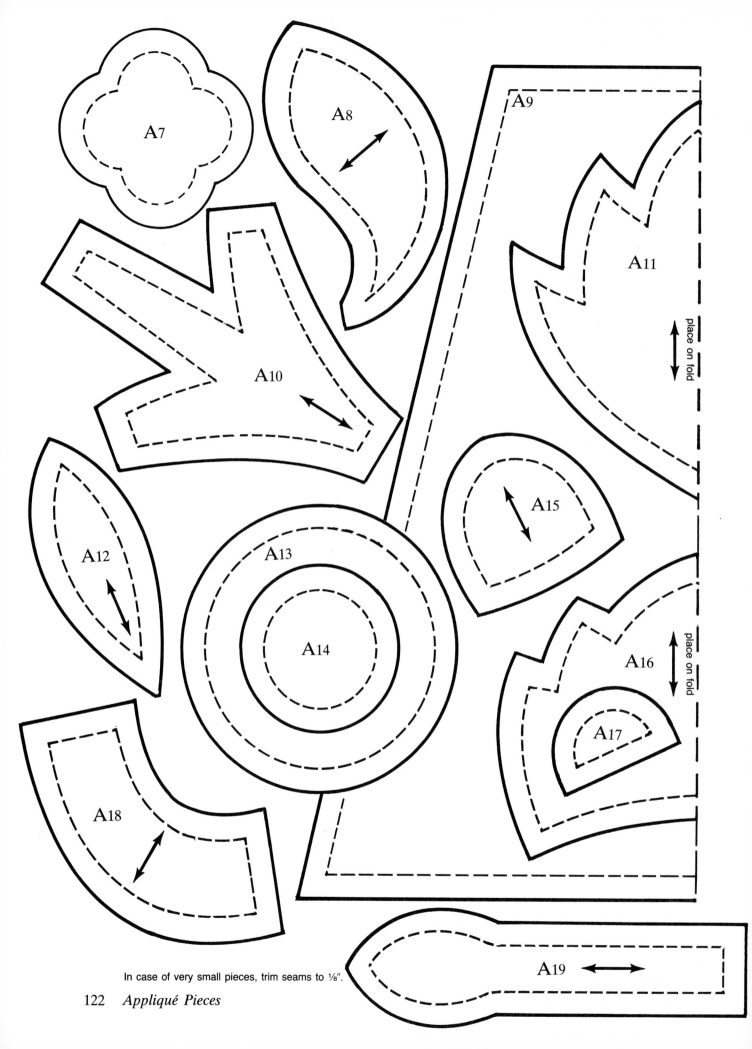

A7

A8

A9

A11

place on fold

A10

A12

A13

A14

A15

A16

place on fold

A17

A18

A19

In case of very small pieces, trim seams to ⅛".

122 *Appliqué Pieces*

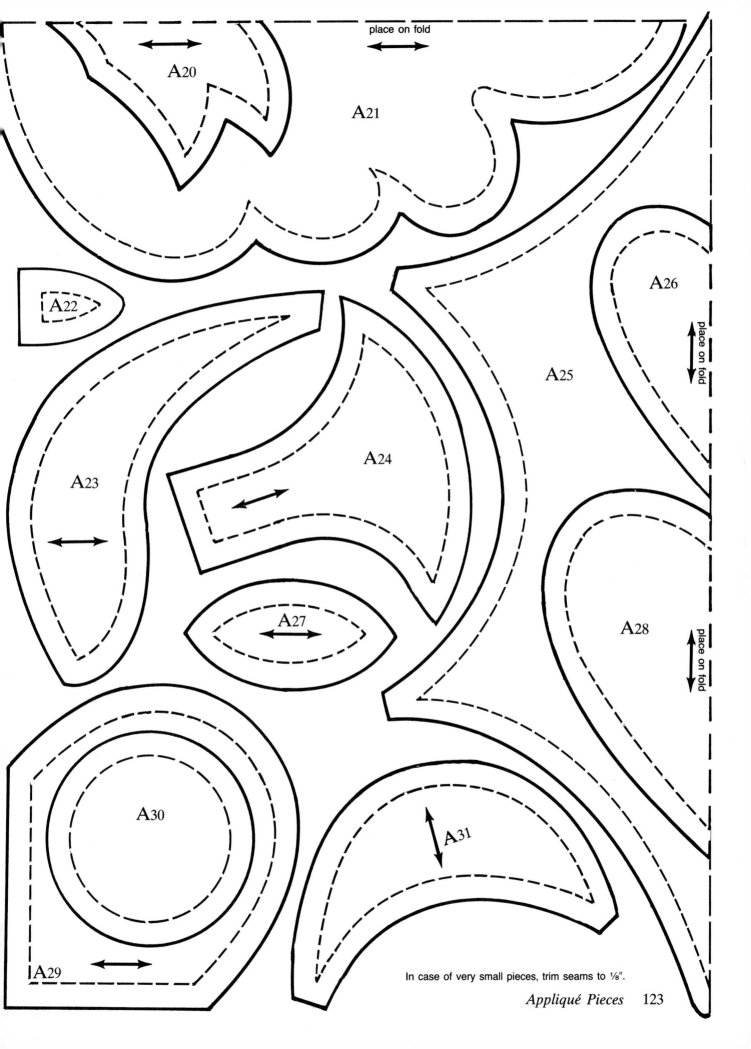

place on fold

A20

A21

A22

A26

place on fold

A25

A23

A24

A27

A28

place on fold

A30

A31

A29

In case of very small pieces, trim seams to ⅛".

*Appliqué Pieces* 123

In case of very small pieces, trim seams to 1/8".

124 *Appliqué Pieces*

# Quilting Patterns

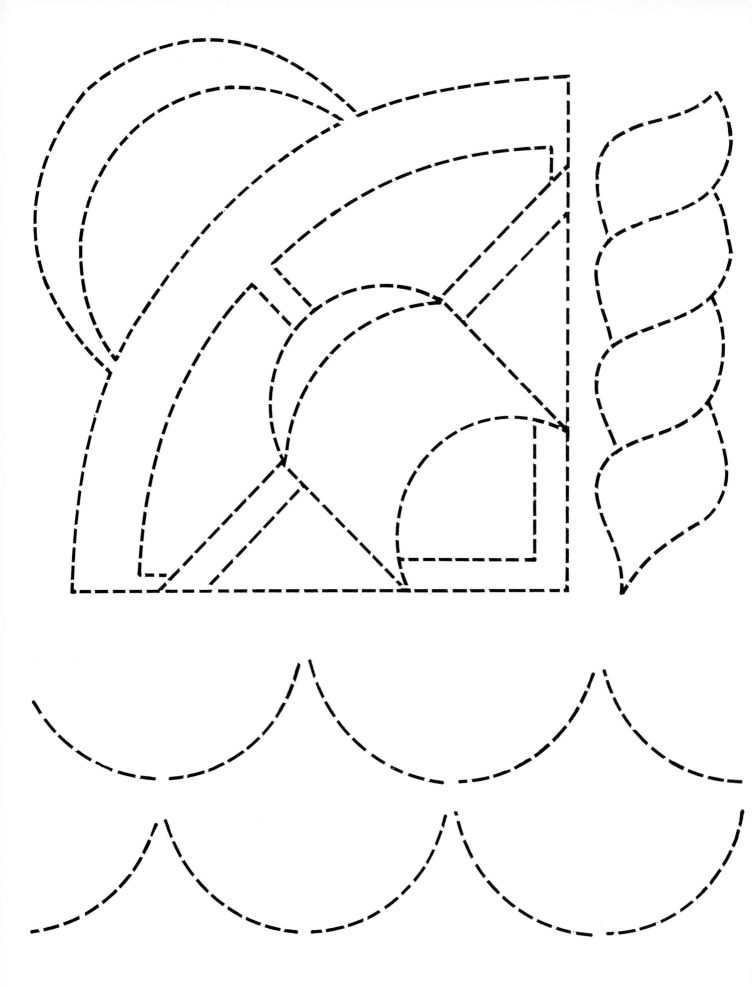

# Glossary

**Appliqué:** Cutout figures sewn to a larger foundation piece of material. Chapter 7, "Applauding Appliqué," examines the options.

**Backing:** The bottom or back layer of a quilt; the underneath side.

**Backstitch:** Used in hand piecing to strengthen a running stitch. Done with a single thread by simply inserting the point of the needle behind the thread each time and coming up ahead. Also used in ending off quilting. When almost out of thread, loop the thread and form a knot close to the fabric. Then backstitch into the quilt top and pull a floater thread through the batting. Come back up about an inch away; clip off.

**Batting:** The filler or middle part of the quilt "sandwich"—the insulation. Today, polyester batting is most widely used and is available in various weights and thicknesses. No matter what type of batting you prefer to use, make sure that it has been bonded.

**Block:** A unit of patchwork, usually in the form of a square, repeated to construct an entire quilt top.

**Block-to-block assembly:** In lap quilting, the process of joining already quilted blocks to form horizontal or vertical rows.

**Borders:** Narrow panels that set off each block in a quilt. The corners of borders may be mitered or squared off with small squares in a contrasting color. Borders may have appliqué accents or can be pieced to create a new design. Borders may also be added to the perimeter of a quilt that needs more length or width. (See page 12.)

**"Cattywampus":** An uneven angle of cloth resulting from a lack of basting or possibly from an unsuccessful quilt connection.

**Chatelaine:** A scissor forget-me-not to be worn around the neck when quilting or doing any needlework. It enables you to "keep it all together"—needles, thread, thimble, and pins.

**Connection:** Joining the three quilting layers—block, batting, backing. In assembly, sewing individual sections together to form the lap-quilting connection.

**Crosshatch:** Two series of parallel lines that intersect. Created on the quilt top as a guide for hand quilting.

**Crazy patch:** A form of patchwork in which odd shapes of fabric are machine-stitched to a foundation block. Embroidery stitches accent seams.

**Dangling thread:** A loose, unknotted thread left in a quilted area to be rethreaded in order to complete quilting once the quilt is assembled.

**"Dog ears":** The triangular extensions formed at the points where diagonal pieces are sewn together. Clipping them relieves the block of excess bulk.

**Edging:** Strips of fabric such as bias tape, used to enclose the perimeter of a quilt. (See page 29.)

**"Eyeball":** Estimating a certain dimension with the experienced eye rather than with a measuring device.

**Flexicurve:** A flexible curve drafting tool, enabling the quilter and seamstress to sew and flip fabric to create curves; may also be used to mark angular lines for quilting. The ½"-wide base accommodates ¼" seams.

**"Fudge":** An irresistible chocolate candy, but in sewing, it means to hedge or cheat a little with fabric!

**Grainline:** The direction of the weave or construction of the yarns in fabric. Warp yarns form the lengthwise pull of the fabric and run parallel to the selvage, while the weft yarns form the right angle.

**Lick:** The process of quickly wetting the fingers to grip layers of fabric better.

**Mitering:** Creating a diagonal seam at the corner of a border to form a right angle. (See page 13.)

**Off hand:** The hand that rests under the quilt, guiding the needle and checking that all three layers have been caught by it. The finger that feels the point of the needle repeatedly should be protected with a thimble, masking tape, a coat of clear nail polish, or the fingertip from an old leather glove.

**Piecing or piecework:** The process of sewing two or more pieces of fabric together.

**Quilt:** Any bed cover with three layers; a sandwich composed of the decorative top, the filler or batting, and the bottom layer or backing. These layers are secured with running stitches (quilting) or with yarn knots (tufting).

**Row-to-row assembly:** In lap quilting, the process of setting together rows of blocks to form a quilt. (See page 20.)

**Setting:** The relationship of one block to the next; the arrangement of blocks that form the quilt top.

**Stencil:** A design for quilting stitches that is transferred to the top, decorative part of a quilt, to provide a stitching guide. (See page 16 for methods of stencil transfer to the fabric. For patterns see page 125.)

**Template:** A pattern made from durable material (cardboard, plastic, sandpaper, or soft vinyl) for patchwork shapes. (See page 9 for instructions on template transfer. For patterns, see page 103.)

**Trapunto:** A softly sculptured effect created by stuffing a design from the back or underside, giving the pattern more dimension.

# Index

*By combining four Offset Maple Leaf blocks, Karen Pervier created this wall hanging,* Georgia on My Mind.

## QUILTS AND DESIGNS

*My experimentation with the blocks
Shadow Dance and Spools resulted in
this wall hanging.*

# Designers & Contributors

Editor: Linda Baltzell Wright
Editorial Assistant: Lenda Wyatt
Copy Chief: Mary Jean Haddin
Design: Diana Smith Morrison
Photography: Courtland W. Richards,
    Mac Jamieson
Art: Don Smith, Samuel L. Baldwin,
    Diana Smith Morrison,
    Janie Farley
Art Director: Bob Nance
Production: Jerry Higdon,
    Jane Bonds